UNDER THE KNIFE

A Beautiful Woman, a Phony Doctor, and a Shocking Homicide

DIANE FANNING

St. Martin's Paperbacks

The names of certain people connected to this story have been changed.

UNDER THE KNIFE

Copyright © 2007 by Diane Fanning.

Cover photo of knife courtesy Corbis Royalty Free. Cover photo of Maria Cruz courtesy Polaris. Cover photo of Dean Faiello courtesy Matthew McDermott/Polaris.

ISBN: 0-312-93952-3
EAN: 9780312-93952-6

Printed in the United States of America

St. Martin's Paperbacks edition / April 2007

St. Martin's Paperbacks are published by St. Martin's Press, 175 Fifth Avenue, New York, NY 10010.

10 9 8 7 6 5 4 3 2 1

*This book is dedicated to Maria Cruz
and to her indomitable spirit in pursuit of the
American Dream*

ACKNOWLEDGMENTS

Reference librarians are an often-unheralded gift from the heavens. They know where to look and how to find the tidbits of information that elude the rest of us.

I owe an enormous debt of gratitude to Sharon Hoyt, reference librarian at the Burlington County public library in New Jersey. Not only did she doggedly pursue questions presented through official channels, but she became so intrigued with the story that she hunted down other documents for me on her personal time. Thank you, Sharon. Thanks, too, to reference librarian Brad Small at the Newark Public Library and to Doug Eldredge of the Newark Preservation Society.

There were a number of medical professionals who provided pieces of Dean Faiello's story or who helped expand my knowledge base with important background information: Dr. Elizabeth Harris and Mary Jo Cunningham at the Center for Cosmetic Surgery in San Antonio; anesthesiologist Dr. David Purchase in New Braunfels, Texas; and Dr. Laurie Polis, Dr. Roy Geronemus, Dr. Ernest Isaacson, and Dr. David Goldschmitt in New York.

I owe a huge debt of appreciation to Dan Kelleher of the Office of Professional Development at the New York City Department of Education, to Barbara Nevins Taylor at New York's Channel 9, to freelance writer Bryon Burrough and to Jeane MacIntosh and Brad Hamilton at the *New York Post*.

Thanks, too, to Barbara Thompson and Edison Alban at the New York County District Attorney's Office in Manhattan, to Mary Price in the correspondence unit of the Manhattan Court Clerks Office—no one can ever sing enough praises for the hard-working folks in clerks' offices everywhere—and to Sister Marguerita Smith, archivist at the Archdiocese of New York.

I offer a standing ovation to Jerry Mitchell and Bart Opsahl, and to Peter Borzotta of Broadway Cares/Equity Fights AIDS.

Thanks to Jenny Kennedy, Rolando Divina, Arthur Mayer, Allie Cramer, criminal profiler Pat Brown, attorneys Kerry Brian Flowers, Margaret Shalley and Ellen Bank, Christopher Giglio of Rubenstein Associates, Steve Baltz of the Osteopathic Medical Board of California. Patrick Merla, Charles Flowers of the Lambda Literary Foundation, Pauline Park of the New York Association for Gender Rights Advocacy and Kim Brinster of the Oscar Wilde Bookshop.

I'd be remiss if I did not offer a whispered thanks to the people who shared their stories with me but requested anonymity. You all were a great help.

I extend a special thank you to Lynette and May Ann at Curves in New Braunfels for quickly conjuring up a pen and paper and a desktop for my use when returned phone calls arrived in the middle of my workout.

I've thanked Joe Cleemann for his excellent editing of other books in the St. Martin's True Crime Library, but this time, I need to acknowledge his assistance in educating me about the intricacies of navigating New York and directing me to the ethnic restaurants on Ninth Avenue where I scored an excellent lunch. For the editing of this book, I extend my appreciation to my new editor, Yaniv Soha.

As always, my deep and abiding gratitude goes to my wonderful agent Jane Dystel and to executive editor Charles Spicer for their continued faith in me.

And I send an ocean of gratitude to Wayne, a specialist in the care and feeding of a writer, who puts up with my nuttiness and keeps coming back for more.

CHAPTER ONE

A PERFECT SPRING DAY DAWNED OVER MANHATTAN ON PALM Sunday, April 13, 2003. Low morning temperatures rose into the 60s and there wasn't a cloud in the sunny blue sky. The tall buildings blocked direct light from most of the sidewalks until the sun reached its pinnacle at noon.

Maria Pilar Cruz emerged from her luxury high rise on West 50th Street to greet the glorious morning. She was a small Filipina—only 4′11″ weighing just 90 pounds—but she was large in energy and ambition. Workouts at Crunch gym and jogs in Central Park made her as fit as a 35-year-old woman could be.

Her drive to succeed led her out of the Philippines eleven years earlier, eventually taking her to New York City in 1998, where she earned an MBA in finance and international banking as well as U.S. citizenship. By 2003, she was a highly regarded financial analyst for Barclays, bringing in an annual salary that approached $200,000.

That year was full of promise for Maria. She planned to go back to school to study for an additional advanced degree. She conspired with family members to plan a fabulous celebration for her parents' fiftieth anniversary. And she anticipated a Christmas visit to the Philippines—her first trip home since arriving in America.

She did not have work or exercise on her mind when she left her apartment building that morning. Her thoughts were on a higher plane. It was time to pay homage to God for the many blessings in her life. She walked a couple of blocks to St. Malachy's Church for 11 A.M. mass.

After the service she stopped by a Duane Reed pharmacy near the corner of 50th and Broadway. She then headed across town past the flapping flags at Rockefeller Center, across Fifth Avenue, then turned right onto Park Avenue heading south. Directly in front of her, the elaborate Helmsley Building blocked the forward progress of the avenue.

When she reached the Helmsley, she took the pedestrian tunnel to the other side to reach the MetLife Building at 200 Park Avenue. She took the elevator and entered the offices of the Barclays Capital asset management group at 1 that afternoon. She went to her desk to retrieve a few files she needed for a team meeting on Monday morning.

At 1:30 she left, stopping in the upscale lobby mall to withdraw $400 from an ATM machine. She would need a big part of that for an appointment later that day. Her medical provider asked her to bring cash.

Maria used her credit card at Grand Central Terminal and walked back home. At her apartment, she spread out her files on the dining table and immersed herself in preparation for the next day. Engrossed in her work, she lost track of time and had to hurry off, leaving her home in greater disarray than usual.

She headed down to Chelsea for her appointment, arriving sooner than she'd anticipated. With time to kill, she stopped to shop at Loehmann's on Seventh Avenue at 16th Street. At 5, she bought a new blouse—size 2—and a pair of size 6 shoes.

She walked a couple of blocks down 16th Street to her

appointment with Dean Faiello. It was not in a conventional medical office—Dean worked out of a friend's apartment. There he had a laser machine to treat a recurring growth in Maria's mouth called black hairy tongue syndrome. She'd paid visits to a number of other doctors and endured numerous scrapings before finding Dean on the Internet early in 2003. She was impressed with his meticulousness and his professional bedside manner. She was also beguiled by his charm.

That day, prior to the removal process, Dean administered a lidocaine injection into Maria's tongue. Like all local anesthetics, this drug had a small tolerance spectrum. Too low a dose and it would not provide the numbness needed. Too high a dose could result in serious complications. The site of the injection amplified the necessity for accuracy. The tongue is a vascular structure—spongy, absorbent matter criss-crossed with an amazing network of capillaries that rush any substance throughout the body at lightning speed.

Reclining on the treatment table waiting for the drug to take effect, Maria heard a ringing in her ears. It was annoying, but did not cause immediate concern. Then she became light-headed. She closed her eyes to stop the room from spinning. It was an unpleasant sensation, but she thought it would pass.

She tasted something acrid and metallic as if she'd bitten down on a piece of aluminum foil stuck to a morsel of barbecued food. An uncomfortable heat surged through her body from head to toe as a bright red flush radiated across her face. The treatments had never made her feel like this before—she didn't like it, but she didn't complain.

At this point—without a word from Maria—a trained anesthesiologist would have known that the patient was in trouble. Either Dean did not notice the coloration in her face or he did not understand its significance.

He didn't know there was a problem until the seizures began. Maria was no longer aware of her surroundings. Without volition, her body tensed and shook. Dean knew that he had to do something, but had no idea what.

An injection of Pentothal, Versed or diazepam could have readjusted the electrical potential in her brain and stopped the manic motion in her muscles. But Dean did not have the education to know. He did not have the drugs he needed. All he knew was that Maria was convulsing again and again as he stood helpless by her side.

He grabbed his phone and called his friend Patty Rosado. She would have the number of the emergency room director at New York University Downtown Hospital, Dr. David Goldschmitt, who lived just a block away from Dean's home in Newark. Patty called David and asked if it was okay to give Dean his home phone number. Then she called Dean back, and gave it to him. Dean wasted no time making the call. He explained the nature of his emergency to David, claiming that the convulsing woman was his friend and asking what he should do.

The doctor was blunt. "Call an ambulance and get her to the hospital," he said.

"She's regaining consciousness now," Dean said. "I'll ask her if she wants to go to the hospital."

"Don't ask her," Dr. Goldschmitt insisted. "Just take her. The seizures will start again. This time they could kill her. Get her to the hospital now."

Without response, Dean hung up the phone. He'd been pushing the boundaries of acceptable behavior for years, but now he stood on the precipice—gazing at a line he should not cross. This was the most pivotal moment of Dean Faiello's life. It was the ultimate test of his character. The right course of action blazoned before him, as clear and obvious as the lights on a runway. At this point, he faltered and he failed—he failed Maria Cruz and failed himself.

Call the authorities and face the consequence of his actions? He was too scared to follow Goldschmitt's advice. He had to ride this out. He could not afford to take her to the hospital. He was in trouble already. Taking Maria in for help would make everything so much worse. As soon as she survived the crisis, they would ask her who did this to her. The moment she uttered his name he was doomed.

David wanted to call for an ambulance himself, but all he knew was that Dean and this woman were in an apartment in Manhattan. He punched star-69 into his phone to reconnect with Dean, but the number was blocked. David was concerned—he didn't think he'd convinced Dean of the situation's urgency.

He felt helpless and frustrated. His career as a physician was founded on saving lives—he worked to that end every day in the emergency room. In the aftermath of 9-11, David had been in the eye of the storm, working unending hours at a hospital close to ground zero. And now he feared a woman was dying and there was nothing he could do. The thought brought back visions of the dead and the dying on that dreadful day less than two years earlier.

Meanwhile, in the makeshift office, Maria's seizures ceased. Dean sighed out his relief, thinking he had weathered the crisis—until he realized that her chest was not rising and falling as it should. She was not breathing. He put his fingers to her wrist, to her throat. She had no pulse. He checked for a heartbeat. He heard not a sound.

He stabbed the number of his accountant, financial advisor and friend Martin Mannert into the telephone. "She had a reaction to lidocaine," he said. "There are no vital signs. No respiration. No pulse. I don't know what to do."

"I'll call 9-1-1," the friend offered.

"No. No, don't do that. I'll take her to St. Vincent's right away." There was a trauma center at St. Vincent's hospital and it was only four and a half blocks away from Dean's makeshift office.

Maria never arrived there. Dean never made the effort.

He panicked at the thought of the cost he would pay—the repercussions that he would suffer—if he did the right thing. He thought of life behind bars. He knew his 6-month plea-bargained sentence on an earlier charge would vanish into thin air if the authorities knew he was still treating patients. Consumed with his own personal peril, he did not spare a moment's concern for the woman who would pay the highest price of all.

He pulled a carry-on suitcase from a closet. It was too small to hold most adults, but Maria was a tiny woman. Now that her natural vivacity was extinguished, she looked smaller than ever. Dean had little trouble folding her still-pliable body into the bag and zipping it shut.

The little wheels whirred smoothly down the hall as Dean eased the suitcase into the elevator. He descended, then jarred the contents as he exited the lift, pulling the beloved daughter of Rudolfo and Irenea Cruz over the gap.

He rolled the suitcase outside to his green SUV. Even with Maria inside, it still weighed less than 100 pounds. For a strong guy like Dean, heaving it into the back of his '96 Jeep Cherokee barely raised a sweat.

He drove through the Holland Tunnel to Newark, New Jersey, taking the tiny Filipina's body to his elegant old home, the former residence of opera diva Madame Maria Jeritza.

Maria Cruz would not rest in peace.

CHAPTER TWO

THAT MONDAY AT BARCLAYS, CONCERN RIPPLED THROUGH the office. Maria did not come to work. She did not call. People in the office called her apartment throughout the day. No one answered the phone. This was so unlike Maria. She was prompt. She was reliable. She never missed work without an explanation.

The next day, still no Maria. Co-worker Martin Davey went to St. Joseph's Home, the boarding house on West 44th Street. He was surprised to discover Maria had moved out a few months earlier. He returned to the office and checked with the human resources department for a new address.

Another co-worker, Mike Reagan, lived closest to Maria's apartment. He agreed to check on her on his way into work on Wednesday morning. He stood outside of her unit with dismay. Stacked before the door were three issues of *The Wall Street Journal*. He rang the bell. He knocked till his knuckles hurt. No Maria.

Back at Barclays, Maria's unexplained absence rattled her supervisor, Hans Christensen. He pulled Maria's file, looked up her emergency contact information and placed a call to her aunt, Rebecca de los Angeles, who lived on the other side of the Upper New York Bay in Jersey City.

The red flags flew immediately for Rebecca. Her

niece had a strong work ethic, an unshakeable sense of responsibility. Something was wrong. She called her nephew Orlando Castillo. Orlando rounded up his brothers, Rafael and Emanuel, and they made their way to West 50th Street.

All hope of an innocent explanation fled at the sight of the newspapers piling up at Maria's door. They found the building manager, but he would not grant access to any tenant's apartment without the assistance of the police.

Orlando and Rafael walked over to the 54th Street station of the New York Police Department. They returned with two female officers. The police women forced the door open. Inside, there were no signs of foul play—nothing to indicate forced entry. Orlando went straight to the spot where Maria stored important papers and discovered that even her passport was in the right place. The police review only confirmed what the emotional family saw: the ordinary sight of a slightly disheveled Spartan apartment, that of a woman who placed little value on material possessions. Maria's purse was missing, as were a pair of gray sneakers. All else appeared to be in place.

IN NEWARK, DEAN FAIELLO WAS STOCKPILING BAGS OF CONcrete. Friends Greg Bach and Mark Ritchey both purchased bags at Home Depot for him. Some were needed for repairs to the home, but Greg noticed the excess and worried about how they were going to dispose of all those heavy sacks when it was time to move. They couldn't be put in the trash. *Just what do you do with leftover bags of concrete?* he wondered. He hoped that moisture didn't turn them into heavy, hardened blocks of dead weight before it was time to get rid of them.

Dean's neighbor Dr. Goldschmitt finally caught up with Dean and asked about the woman who was in medical distress.

"She came out of her convulsions, was fine and went home," Dean said.

David Goldschmitt felt an immense sense of relief.

Dean ran into Martin Mannert, the accountant friend he called on April 13. Dean said Maria was fine. "I took her to St. Vincent's," he said, "and all was well."

MARIA'S BROTHER JUN, A 42-YEAR-OLD ENGINEER, AND HER sister Tes Lara, a 39-year-old dentist, landed at JFK International Airport on Good Friday, April 18, at 3 P.M. Weary from their long flight from the Philippines, they were dismayed to find that Maria was not there to meet them. They waited until 5 before contacting other family members, looking for their little sister.

Missing, they were told. *Maria was missing*. Jun and Tes learned that, while they were in flight to the States, other family members spent the day calling hospitals to no avail. When their cousins wanted to file a missing persons report, police told them to hold off for a week, the standard waiting time for a missing adult. Tes and Jun were not willing to linger. It was time to take the next step—to push it, if necessary.

With their uncle, Jose Navarro, Maria's siblings went to the Midtown North NYPD station on 54th Street to file the report. Initially, Maria landed on the long unfortunate list of the missing—just one more lost individual of the 18,400 people who'd disappeared in New York City in the first five months of 2003. Jose convinced Officer Ponce that Maria's disappearance was not an ordinary case of someone not wanting to be found—the circumstances justified an immediate investigation.

Ponce referred the family to Detective Joseph Della Rocca. The investigator accompanied Jose, Tes and Jun to Maria's fourteenth-floor apartment. After speaking to the building manager, they entered Maria's home.

Again, there was no obvious evidence of foul play—no forced entry, no indication of a struggle—but nothing felt right. For Tes and Jun, the subtle signs were alarming. Meticulous and neat, Maria would never leave her place in such disarray unless she intended to return immediately. Soiled dishes piled in the sink. Fresh grapes lay out on the counter. Papers sprawled across the kitchen table. Leftovers in the refrigerator and open blinds in one window further indicated that Maria did not intend to be away from her apartment for long.

None of it made any sense.

Hoping against hope, the family made the rounds of Manhattan hospitals. They looked in on every Jane Doe in each facility. Still, no sign of Maria. No word from Maria.

On Sunday, Jose and Jun looked on the Internet for clues. They found a credit report in which Maria used the name Marisol. They found other documents from the time just after she got her United States citizenship with this name, too. Once again, calls went out to all the hospitals in the area. This time, the family asked for Marisol Cruz.

ACROSS THE HUDSON RIVER, DEAN FAIELLO PREPARED HIS home for sale. He had lived there for seventeen years. Before Maria's death, he had faced serious financial problems. Now impending foreclosure made the sale mandatory. Unaware of anything but Dean's economic distress, friends and neighbors pitched in to help the adorable, charismatic doctor with home improvements for the sale, and then with cleanup for the move.

Dean's current boyfriend, Greg Bach, spent May 27, 2003, removing discarded items from the home and depositing them in a rented Dumpster on the sidewalk. At 2 that afternoon, he spotted Dean in the carriage house. The upper level of the old white building was rented out as an apartment. The lower level, where Dean now stood, was used as a garage and, although it was narrow, it had enough room to house three cars. Now, though, a little red wagon could not have parked inside. Dean stored belongings there as he emptied the house, packing the space full. Boxes and furniture were piled from floor to ceiling, wall to wall. Only a narrow passageway to the storage closet at the back of the structure remained open, and it was not easy to negotiate.

Dean filled a large plastic container with bags of Quikrete concrete mix. "What are you doing?" Greg asked.

"Gotta fix the plumbing."

Odd answer, Greg thought, and shrugged as he went back to work. Dean—a man who preferred coaxing acquaintances or hiring professionals to doing any hard labor himself—worked with surprising dedication in the carriage house. He mixed concrete and poured enough to build a platform in the storage closet. He slid a suitcase—enclosed in a garbage bag and taped shut—into the wet concrete. In it were the earthly remains of Maria Cruz. The suitcase wiggled as it rested on a semi-solid platform of gray. Dean pushed the container down into the sludge as far as he could, then covered it with more concrete.

Around 4, Greg stepped into the doorway of the carriage house and saw Dean smoothing out the surface with a trowel. "What are you doing? Can I help?" Greg asked.

Dean flipped into instant hostility. "Would you get outta here? Leave me alone. Go away. Go do something else."

Greg went back into the house. He thought Dean's behavior was bizarre, but blamed it on the recent deterioration of their relationship. Lately, Dean flew off the handle at the slightest provocation. At this point, Greg found his tantrums almost amusing.

On a perverse impulse, Greg returned to the garage,

intending to agitate Dean again. He stood behind him and asked, "Whatcha doin'?"

Again Dean went off on him. As he ranted, Greg laughed in Dean's face.

THE NEXT DAY, THE SALE OF THE HOUSE IN NEWARK CLOSED. With a little help from his friends, Dean sold the home for $423,000—close to the initial asking price of $450,000 and substantially more than what he paid for it.

Dean moved in to the third-floor apartment of Mark Ritchey's house on Highland Avenue, just two blocks up from the corner of Elwood and Ridge where Dean's former residence stood. Mark's home—with its large round columns and strikingly decorated porch and lawn—sported an artsy look that set it apart from the more traditional appearance of its stodgy neighbors.

The new owner of Dean's home—a property surrounded by fifteen-foot-high wrought-iron fences enclosing two residential buildings and a carriage house—thought he had gotten a good deal on an historic home. He had no idea of the history hidden in a sloppy slab of concrete in the storage closet of the carriage house. No clue that an American dream had died and lay buried only yards from where he and his girlfriend slept.

CHAPTER THREE

THE PHILIPPINES POSSESS A RICH TRADITION OF FOLKLORE. Maria Cruz was born in an environment filled with folk tales, passed down orally from one generation to the next. It was a heritage she shared with all Filipino children, whether they were born on the islands or in Hong Kong, the United States or elsewhere.

One story that speaks strongly to their pride and sense of uniqueness is a tale of the creation of man. God molded the first man and popped him into His celestial oven, the story claims. He left this first creation in the oven too long. This man was dark and overdone. God placed him in Africa.

God tried again. This time, He did not leave His creation in the oven long enough. This man was pale and pasty, and God placed him in Europe. On the third attempt, God got it just right. A man with golden skin—perfectly baked. God placed this man in the Philippines.

The golden child, Maria Pilar Cruz, came to earth on March 9, 1968. Her parents, Rudolfo and Irenea Cruz, had five children—one boy and four girls. Maria was nicknamed Ate Pipay. Based on regional tradition, this name indicated that she was the family's fourth daughter. The Cruzes raised their children in the Manila area of the Republic of the Philippines.

The country encompasses more than 7,000 tropical islands, stretching more than 1,100 miles through the southwest Pacific Ocean. Some of these land masses are nothing more than piles of jagged rock or dank swamplands. In fact, 4,300 of the islands don't even have names.

The total land mass is roughly equivalent to the combined size of Wisconsin and Michigan, but the population easily outstrips those two states. At the time of Maria's birth, more than 43 million people occupied the 730 inhabited islands of the Republic.

The main islands are places of stark contrasts. Sharp volcanic peaks rise as high as 9,692 feet above sea level. Rushing rivers plunge through forests filled with monkeys, bats, deer, wild hogs, pygmy buffalo, crocodiles, giant pythons, mouse deer and all manner of lizards and birds. In the lowlands, the wilderness yields to cultivated fields of rice, sugar, coconut palms, pineapples, sweet potatoes, abaca—Manila hemp—and more.

During Maria's childhood, 70 percent of the population earned their living through agriculture. This gave the island nation much in common with its neighbors in Asia.

There were factors though, that set them apart. More than three centuries of Spanish control of the Philippines created a nation where four-fifths of the population belonged to the Roman Catholic Church, making it the only Christian country in the Far East.

Religion is more than a quiet matter of faith for most Filipinos. It dominates their lives, their families and their communities. That holds true for more than just the nation's Catholics. When both Christianity and Islam arrived to the Philippines, those doctrines were superimposed over ancient traditions and became entwined in the cultural identities of the people.

Whether Catholic, Moslem, Protestant, Buddhist or animist, the rituals and ceremonies of their belief touch every day of the lives of most Filipinos. It also gives rise to many festivals throughout the islands, providing a host of multi-cultural reasons for all-out celebration.

Maria was born into a society where the Malay tradition of equality between men and women was a dominating force. The strong presence of Roman Catholicism over the centuries had at one time restrained some of that tradition, but by the time of Maria's birth, the power of that oppression had greatly diminished.

In most Asian cultures at the time of Maria's youth, the man of the house had undisputed authority over his household. In the Philippines, however, marriage was as close to an equal partnership between husband and wife as is found in Western countries. A woman's right to inherit property was never questioned. Education and literacy levels for women tended to be higher than those for men. As in the Western world, though, the country continued to struggle with making equal pay for equal work a reality. A woman's ability to advance in her career lagged behind that of a man.

Equal to the power of religion in Filipino life is the concept of *kapwa*. Translated from the original Tagalog, it means "shared being," and it's demonstrated in a strong desire for connection with others, and the belief that each person is inseparable from those who surrounded him. Everything—from joy to sorrow, from the mundane to the sublime—is meant to be shared.

The third force shaping Filipino society—and perhaps the strongest one of all—is the pivotal role of family. It provides strength, stability and security, extending to aunts, uncles, cousins, godparents, sponsors or patrons and close family friends. This all-compassing definition of family creates the social units of Filipino civilization. Rather than class structure, the primary identification of each individual is his familial group.

With the dominance of this structure comes the obligation of patronage. It is expected that family members receive preferential treatment in hiring. In fact, at many businesses, collective bargaining agreements specifically include this in company policy. The practice creates a cohesive work force, but it also leads to the abuse of privilege. This dark side flourished within the régime of Ferdinand Marcos. Filipinos elected him as president in 1965. The moment he took office he packed the government with appointments based on patronage with a total disregard for skill sets or knowledge level.

When Maria was a 1-year-old, he ran for re-election with promises of rice and roads. Marcos was the first president to win a second election since 1935 when self-rule was initiated in the island nation.

After that success, the domestic situation turned sour for Marcos. Filipinos opposed to the United States' presence in their country—and to the government's support of U.S. policy in Vietnam—led active protests. The Communist Party of the Philippines and the Moslem separatist movement grew stronger and spread unrest throughout the islands.

In 1972, Marcos declared martial law, claiming that anarchy was near. The following year—when his two-term limit was due to expire—Marcos suspended the constitution, dissolved the congress, arrested his political opposition and ended the long tradition of a free press. The new constitution anointed Marcos president and prime minister, and it postponed elections for an indefinite period.

Under his rule, a culture of corruption swamped the island. While those in power plundered the economy, Marcos spoke of the need for self-sacrifice. Comfortably entrenched, Marcos lifted martial law in 1981, but retained sufficient power to control a farcical presidential election, which he won with ease.

Benigno Aquino, Marcos' chief political opponent, returned to the Philippines in 1983 after years in exile in the United States. He was shot in the back of the head minutes after his arrival at Manila International Airport. His assassination sparked the downfall of Ferdinand Marcos.

Corazon Aquino, widow of the fallen politician, became the focal point of the opposition to Marcos. In an attempt to regain political legitimacy, Marcos declared an early presidential election in February 1986. Corazon ran against Marcos, and though observers from the U.S. and an official government commission disagreed on the election results, the national assembly ultimately declared Marcos the winner.

Tens of thousands of civilians took to the streets in protest led by the military, who stood in opposition to the actions of the legislative body. Marcos, his family and his cronies fled to Hawaii on United States Air Force planes as Corazon Aquino became president. She was a role model for Filipinas all over the world. Maria Cruz was 18 years old at the time—and the impact of that woman's rise to power strengthened Maria's ambition and empowered her to succeed.

CHAPTER FOUR

MARIA'S BROTHER, JUN, FOLLOWED IN HIS FATHER'S FOOT-steps and became an engineer. Her older sister, Tes, studied dentistry. Maria, too, continued on to college. It was expected in their family, which, like that of most Filipinos, placed a high value on education. They believed it was the path to upward mobility both socially and economically.

Maria chose Miriam College in Quezon City for her undergraduate schooling. A recent addition to the Philippine landscape, Quezon City was President Manuel Luis Quezon's vision of a town where the common man could find his place with dignity. To achieve his dream, the president purchased a vast estate and chartered the city in 1939. It became the capital of the Philippines in 1948.

Quezon City is nestled in rolling hills, ten miles from Manila. Spacious parks and tree-lined boulevards beautify the town. One neighborhood, Loyola Heights, an upper middle class residential area, became home to Maria's alma mater in 1952.

At the urging of the diocese, the sisters of Maryknoll Congregation in New York founded the institution as a teacher-training program in 1926. It became Maryknoll College in 1952 and developed into a liberal arts facility committed to the formation of women leaders and teachers.

In 1977, the Sisters turned ownership and management of the school over to Filipino laity and it was re-named Miriam College after the Aramaic name for the mother of Jesus. The new administrators established three major centers for curriculum development, research and community outreach: the Environmental Studies Institute; the Center for Peace Education; and the Women & Gender Institute.

When Maria arrived on campus, she entered a world where Christianity, specifically Catholicism, was central to the educational experience. The core value statement read: "Miriam College is committed to the values of truth, justice, peace and the integrity of creation." It was also an environment where women's ambitions were nurtured—where they were encouraged to strive and excel.

Maria took that philosophy to heart. She majored in Communications Arts and was considered the best student in her class. She didn't tell her family that she'd earned *cum laude* honors. She surprised them with that revelation when she walked across the stage and accepted her diploma.

For a short while after graduation, she worked for the Ayala Corporation, a holding company. Ayala, founded in 1834, was one of the largest and most respected businesses in the Philippines.

But before the year was over, Maria decided to fulfill her ultimate dream—she moved to the United States. Her transition was easier than that of many immigrants because of the absence of a language barrier. Although Filipino—based on the native Tagalog dialect—is the official language of the nation, it is not spoken or even understood by large portions of the country. English is spoken in schools, the government and in business, making the estimated 86 million people living in the Philippines in 2004 the third largest group of English-speaking people in the world.

Maria's first stop in her new country was Houston, Texas, where she worked for Citibank. As big as it was, the Bayou City did not possess the hustle or import in the financial community that Maria desired. Her ambition drove her to the world capital of global business—New York City. She arrived in the city of her dreams in 1993 through a job transfer at Citibank.

There, she enrolled at Fordham, the Jesuit University of New York. The Graduate School of Business Administration was located at Lincoln Center near Central Park, not far from St. Joseph's Home—the boarding house on West 44th Street that she now called home. It was a modest structure, designed as a model tenement in the late nineteenth century. The minuscule apartments offered only tight quarters for families, but the building's saving grace was its enormous courtyard, built to provide air and light and to serve as a safe place for children to play.

At the time Maria moved in, the entrance was cramped and awkward to negotiate. A set of steps jutted out from the building. A tall wrought-iron fence pressed against the stairs on three sides. When she opened the gate, she had to step up immediately and then bend down to pull it shut. The steps led from the sidewalk to the outside doors. On that landing, a statue of St. Joseph perched on a pedestal in the corner. Passers-by often mistook the building for a church and paused to genuflect and pray. More steps rose up between the outer and inner doors. In that tiny foyer, a cheerful, bright-colored tile mosaic offered a warm welcome to residents and visitors.

Catholic women dominated the population of this Church-owned facility, although other religions were represented as well. Women from India, Central America, the United States and all across the globe called St. Joseph's home, though Filipinas outnumbered the rest.

Most of the women remained for long periods of time, the rooms full year after year.

By Manhattan standards, that section of 44th Street was a quiet oasis. Trees lined the sidewalk—each one surrounded by a tiny wrought-iron fence encircling a bed of colorful tulips, daffodils and jonquils in the spring. The bustle of Ninth Avenue, though, was just a block away. Dubbed Ethnic Avenue by New Yorkers, this stretch of real estate was known for its exotic restaurants—Brazilian, Turkish, Afghan, Mexican, Jamaican, Balinese and more.

Maria graduated with honors from the esteemed business school at Fordham. She now held an MBA in finance and international banking. Family members said that she was very happy with her position at Citibank. In 2001, though, Barclays Capital made aggressive moves to pick up personnel from other businesses. They staged a futile and much publicized raid against Credit Suisse First Boston in February in an attempt to lure away senior bond executives. The more modest attempt at Citigroup netted a win for Barclays, and Maria felt her best choice was to go with her team. She entered the new company many steps up the ladder on her way to becoming a certified financial analyst. Barclays offered a world well suited to Maria—or to any woman pursuing success. It was a corporate environment where meritocracy was central. A woman with Maria's ambition was destined to stand out.

Despite her improved financial status, Maria remained at St. Joseph's Home for some time, continuing to attend mass nearly every day. Her church of choice, St. Malachy's—the actors' chapel—was rich in history. The Church founded the parish in 1902, and erected the neo-gothic building in 1903.

When the Theatre District sprang up in the area in the 1920s, the church became a haven for actors, dancers and musicians. St. Malachy's offered atypical times for worship—a 5 P.M. mass before performances and a late mass at midnight, 2 A.M. or even 4 A.M. to accommodate entertainers and the people who labored backstage on Broadway.

Douglas Fairbanks and Joan Crawford were married at St. Malachy's. A final tribute to Rudolph Valentino there filled the sanctuary and spilled out into the streets. Spencer Tracy, Perry Como, Irene Dunne, Bob and Dolores Hope, Danny Thomas, Ricardo Montalban, Jimmy Durante and Florence Henderson were among the many stars who worshiped there.

Inside the doors, celebrity was left behind and a hush descended as sculpted marble columns ascended to great heights, supporting the chapel's three arches. The two side arches had lower deep blue ceilings sprinkled with golden stars. The middle arch rose in gothic splendor to a carved ceiling. The focal point was an ornate altar backed by a painted mural of Christ on the cross.

Dark wooden pews arced out from the front of the altar. Stained glass windows flanked each side. The architectural splendor provided the heady, tremulous sensation of standing in the presence of God.

DESPITE HER IMPROVED SITUATION, MARIA DID NOT, AT FIRST, make any expenditure to improve her own lifestyle. Instead, she spent her money on others. She treated her parents to an anniversary cruise in the Bahamas. She splurged on relatives when they traveled from the Philippines to visit her in New York. She was known to munch on an apple for lunch and open a can of okra for dinner when she ate on her own, but would not hesitate to pay for Broadway plays and expensive Apple Tours excursions for family members. Once the first choice of tourists to New York, now defunct after a collision with a Hell's Kitchen resident.

In the romance department things blew hot, then ice cold. For four intense months, she had a serious relationship with Bill Morgan. When he moved to Chicago, they agreed that it was over. Emotionally, though, Maria had a hard time letting go. She contacted him later with a proposal that she follow him to the Windy City. She dropped that idea when Bill told her he planned to marry someone else.

In 2002, Maria took the next step to molding her vision of a perfect life: She became a naturalized United States citizen. In May of that year, she took a trip to Houston for a family wedding. Her parents flew in from the Philippines for the occasion. The reunion was short but sweet. Rudolfo and Irenea had no way of knowing that it would be the last time they would ever see their daughter.

At Christmas time, Maria took in the glorious display at Rockefeller Center. She loved the pageantry of Christmas in Manhattan, but vowed that when the holiday rolled around the next time, she would celebrate in her native land.

No country on earth has a longer celebration of Christmas than the one in the Philippines. Every household is adorned with the bright, colorful parol—the national symbol of the Star of Bethlehem. For nine mornings, Catholic families gather at their local churches for a dawn mass. Outside, vendors fill the air with the tantalizing scent of traditional holiday treats.

After mass, families gather round to purchase and consume *bibingka*—a sweet rice cake resembling a Western pancake topped with grated coconut—and *puto bumbong*, a rice and water batter baked in a special clay pot lined with banana leaves and topped with slices of *kesong puti*, a white cheese, and *itlog na maalat*, salted duck eggs. The thought of these native concoctions made Maria's mouth water, and she began to plan her first trip back to the Philippines in more than ten years.

As 2002 came to a close, so did Maria's decade-long stay at St. Joseph's Home. She moved seven blocks away to a luxury studio apartment on the fourteenth floor of a high-rise complex with a uniformed doorman.

In January of 2003, Maria Cruz surfed the Internet and made a fatal decision. She scheduled her first appointment with Dean Faiello.

CHAPTER FIVE

DEAN FAIELLO WAS BORN AT CLARA MAAS HOSPITAL IN Belleville, New Jersey, on August 31, 1959. Sam and Carmel Faiello brought their first child home to Newark, where the family lived in the home of Dean's widowed maternal grandmother, Ada.

The year Dean turned three, he and his parents moved into their own home at 9 Cedar Avenue in Madison, a small, affluent town close to New York City. Another change occurred in the Faiello household that year—Dean's sister Debra was born.

To the children, the world revolved around their mother. She stayed at home and devoted her life to her kids. Like all the women in her family, Dean's mother was of diminutive stature—just 5'3", a couple of inches taller than her own mother. To her children, though, she thrust sky-high—a tower of strength. When they spoke to her, she focused in on their words, looked them directly in the eye and made them feel like the most special people in the world. Her smile lingered in Dean's mind. It was a warm and radiant smile that filled her entire face.

Her influence extended beyond the children. Carmel affected the mood of those in any room she entered. No one could ignore her presence. She was loved for her kindness and empathy.

Carmel sent her children off to school in clean, fresh-pressed outfits with lunch money in hand. She made sure they were on time for class. She was active in the PTA, helping organize school fairs and pot-luck dinners. When the kids returned home each day, they knew she would be there waiting with snacks, ready to listen to their stories about school.

Despite the chaos of having two young children at home, Carmel maintained a fastidious appearance. She kept her nails manicured, her hair styled, her make-up impeccable and her clothing always neat and well suited to each occasion.

She took just as much care with her home. Carmel had a keen eye for design and never overlooked the slightest detail in pulling together a picture-perfect room. She painted woodwork, hung wallpaper and added coordinated accessories in a cycle of redecoration that never seemed to end. She added personal touches to the rooms of her children. Both had desks for doing homework. She put up a shelf for Dean's collection of Hardy Boys books and hung another in Debra's room for her ever-growing collection of athletic trophies.

She kept the home full of candles, plants and tasteful knick-knacks all year round. When Christmas time came, she threw herself into the spirit with decorations and handmade ornaments. Long before it was the norm, she strung tiny white lights everywhere to make her house glow.

Carmel was devoted to her children. Every one of their accomplishments made her beam with pride. A good report card from Dean, a trophy from Debra—they laid their offerings at her feet for the reward of her smile. If anyone hurt her children, that smile turned into a scowl, and her protective maternal instincts rose to the fore.

She seemed to hold the whole world in her hands, but

there was one thing she could not shape into her pleasant ideal of a life well-lived—her husband.

Sam's narcissistic appetite for manipulation made Carmel's control over anything seem precarious. He used his wife and children to stroke his ego and inflate his sense of self-importance. When they didn't cater to his needs, there was hell to pay. Verbal and physical abuse were common. Carmel intervened, interrupting beatings, brushing away tears and holding the children tight till the pain faded away. But fortunately for the family, their interaction with Sam was minimal—he spent most of his time elsewhere.

When he did come home, everyone waited timidly at the garage door to greet him. Like all kids raised in the sixties, Dean and Debra loved their TV shows. Their favorites were typical fare: *My Favorite Martian*, *Green Acres*, *Lost in Space* and *Gilligan's Island*. But when it was time for Dad to come home, they'd better not be watching television. Their place was beside the garage door, waiting for the return of the family breadwinner. If they were not there to greet him, he was furious. Even when respectfully met at the door, Sam shut himself in the den away from his family after just a brief moment of interaction.

Dean carried items to his Dad's den for his mother on occasion. The biggest life lesson he remembered learning from his father was how to make a vodka martini. Dean followed his father's instruction with care. He coated the ice cubes with vermouth, pouring the excess away, leaving only the ice cubes to flavor the vodka—in the Faiello household the martini was gently stirred, never shaken. Then, according to his father's mood and the supplies on hand, he added a twist or an olive. After serving Sam, Dean left the room as soon as he could.

Carmel did all she could to counteract the toxic atmosphere created by her hostile, demanding husband. When he was gone, she created an environment of peace, an oasis of love. When he blew in like a hurricane, she did her best to keep her children out of his way.

From 1966 through 1970, summers were a special escape for Dean and Debra. They spent the entire season at the home of their paternal grandfather, Carmine. He and his second wife, Emma, lived just a couple hundred feet from the beach in South Seaside Park. The unincorporated town was across from Toms River on the Barnegat Bay on an Ocean County barrier island in southern New Jersey.

Carmine, an immigrant from Italy, owned the town's water utility, South Seashore Water Company. Rumors circulated that he was connected to the Mob. Whether they were based on fact or ethnic stereotype, they persist even to today.

Emma worked on the beach selling admission badges during the season. Dean and Debra left Madison on Memorial Day weekend and spent nearly every day of their break from school frolicking beachside—cooling off in the waves, baking in the sun.

This world of playtime fantasy, made up of miles of white sand, filled their summers with seagulls and horseshoe crabs. Up on the boardwalk, the fresh ocean breeze mingled with the acrid smell of the creosote-soaked boards and the sweet scent of cotton candy. They rode the roller coaster, Tilt-A-Whirl and bumper cars until they were exhausted. They journeyed through the haunted house and the house of mirrors and down water slides. They collected pinwheel art and stuffed animals. They played Skee-Ball, ring toss and other games of chance that tempted them along the length of the broad boardwalk. They stuffed their tummies with hot pretzels, cold custard, Orange Julius and deep-fried zeppola—an Italian fried dough concoction drenched in powdered sugar.

Then Labor Day came and Dean and Debra's world of limitless freedom and fun came to a screeching halt. Once again, it was time for school work—and the harder job of avoiding their father's wrath.

CHAPTER SIX

DEAN WAS 12 YEARS OLD AND DEBRA WAS 9 WHEN THEIR parents first separated. Sam moved out of the home on 9 Cedar Avenue. He consulted an attorney who advised him to move back into the home, or his wife could divorce him on grounds of abandonment. The lawyer convinced him that a no-fault divorce would leave him in a better position—he would lose fewer of his assets, and his alimony and child support payments would be lower.

So weeks after leaving, Sam returned. He forced his way in and reclaimed 9 Cedar Avenue as his own. For Dean's mother, this started the divorce clock all over again. At that time, to legally end a marriage, a couple needed to live apart for eighteen months. Now, Carmel had no choice. She had to leave the home at once to free herself of the man who made her and her children miserable.

Carmel told Dean and Debra to pack their things. They had to move from the only place either child could remember calling home. Dean stood in his bedroom in a daze. He stared in his sock drawer not knowing which colors to take and which to leave behind. He didn't even know how long he would be gone or if he would ever return.

As he stood stock still, incapable of taking any action, Sam entered his room. "Can I help you?" he asked.

Dean glared at him. How could he offer to help his son

pack his clothes and leave his home in the middle of the night? He wanted to say, "Sure, you can help me—by leaving my sister and my mother and me alone." Instead, he just shook his head.

The three found refuge at grandmother Ada's home in Newark. She was living alone in a small apartment with only a living room, a bedroom and a kitchen. Now, four people occupied the tiny space. Despite the challenge and the loss of privacy, Ada did all she could to make her daughter and grandchildren feel welcome.

Ada slept on the sofa—a situation that embarrassed Dean. He offered to take her place, but she would not give it up. In the sole bedroom, his mother slept on an uncomfortable cot. Dean offered her his place in the bed where he and Debra slept but she would not even consider it. He and his sister had school to attend, she told him; they needed to sleep well. Watching the sacrifice of his mother and grandmother night after night fed the flames of anger and resentment that Dean felt toward his father.

Every morning, Carmel drove Dean and Debra to school in Madison. Every afternoon, she drove back to pick them up and bring them to the loving but minuscule apartment. Dean's mother struggled with depression over her situation—the overcrowded home, the endless negotiations and waiting for the divorce papers. For the first time in her life, she let herself go. Her hair hung limp for days at a time, her fingernails became chipped and ragged, her clothing draped from her body. Compared to a lot of women, she still looked great. But for Carmel, the appearance was definitely sub-par.

The largest room in the apartment was the kitchen, where Italian tradition made meal preparation a central part of every day. After school, Dean sat down at the long white Formica table to do his homework while his grandmother and mother bustled over the hot stove. Surrounded by school books and the delicious aroma of home cooking, he studied hard, nibbling on the treats they set before him.

Outside, the neighborhood was not the suburban sanctuary of Dean and Debra's earlier life. Gone were the broad manicured yards—these houses were separated by only the width of the driveway. Gone were the trees they used to climb and the vast expanses of grass where they could run and play. Here, concrete and a garage adorned the backyards of most homes. Gone were safe streets where children tossed balls and rode bikes. In the city, the streets were busy and dangerous. Gone were the pleasant window views of sweeping lawns covered with lush, green grass and dotted with trees, flowers and shrubs. Here the only sight was the wall of another structure, blocking the sun.

Dean passed through his early adolescence with no strong father figure—or any man—in his life. The only male in an otherwise female household, he lived in an apartment complex filled with single mothers and widows.

After two and a half years of exile in these crowded conditions, the divorce was at last final. Now, mother and children could return to their home in Madison and reconstruct their lives. Sam was not around much, but when he stopped for a visit, he belittled his children non-stop, calling Dean fat, insolent, effeminate, vain and unmotivated, despite the fact that Dean had the best grade point average in his class. Sam never offered a word of praise for Dean's achievements.

He did not spare Debra either. He told Debra, a star athlete in high school, that she was fat, lazy, unappreciative, impolite and spoiled. Looking back on the accomplishments of these children, the way their father described them was preposterous. But, for these teenagers, each jab poked through their veneer of self-confidence. The emotional impact was devastating.

Still, Dean continued to work hard on his studies and to be active in extracurricular activities. He was president of the National Honor Society, the literary magazine editor, president of the student ad-hoc committee, president of the annual arts festival and a member of the ski club. Dean's classmates voted him "most likely to succeed." According to the yearbook, he liked "skiing, tennis, Dylan, snow and carpeted lockers." "Over-dramatic poetry and locked doors" annoyed him. He promised himself and his classmates that he would become an engineer.

His charming ways and good looks drew other students into his orbit. His friends called him Dino. Every year, a new bevy of girls developed crushes on the dark-haired, olive-skinned hunk of a boy in their midst.

He learned at a young age that certain privileges beyond popularity accompanied his remarkable good looks. He found that he often got a free pass on issues that would have sunk a homelier person, in the social set of his peers. At times, that bothered Dean; but, for the most part, he allowed the preferential treatment to enhance his enjoyment of life. He seemed to believe that his good looks could get him out of any tricky situation.

Dean graduated from Madison High School in 1977. He then attended Rensselaer Polytechnic Institute, a school established in 1824 in Troy, New York. The purpose in its creation was "instructing persons, who may choose to apply themselves, in the application of science to the common purposes of life." When Dean matriculated at Rensselaer, it comprised five schools: Architecture, Engineering, Humanities and Social Science, Management and Science. Noted alumni of the institution included Washington Roebling, engineer of the Brooklyn

Bridge; Raymond Tomlinson, who put the @ in email addresses; Sheldon Roberts of the "Traitorous Eight" who created Silicon Valley; and Bobby Farrelly, director, writer and producer of *There's Something About Mary*.

Dean, however, was not destined for their glory. His commitment to change the world through engineering hit the wall of hard work and died on impact. Living away from home, he didn't have the benefit of his mother's encouragement and discipline to keep him on track. He possessed enough ability and intelligence to succeed, but without Carmel's constant input, he did not have the motivation to excel. He dropped out after five semesters and drifted around from job to job after leaving the school. His father's prophecy seemed to be fulfilling itself.

CHAPTER SEVEN

BY THE MID-EIGHTIES, DEAN WAS OUT OF THE CLOSET AND openly gay. He was also HIV positive. When Christopher Buczek first saw Dean, lust hit him with chaotic intensity. He pursued Dean with single-minded desire, and a torrid romance began.

Christopher told Bryan Burrough, who interviewed him for *Vanity Fair*: "I was one of a long line of people who were obsessed with Dean." He added, "The real thing that drew people to Dean was that soft-spoken manner. He knew just what to say and what not to say. You know, he was like an expert at creating infatuation. For years, he just kept circulating around in my bloodstream, like a virus."

Despite his obsession, Christopher also thought Dean was very shallow. At the time, though, Dean was only 23 years old. Finding any male in that late adolescent age range with any real depth would be a confounding challenge.

Dean's engineering dreams were dead and he floundered around for an alternative way to make a living. He danced a few gigs at New York go-go bars. He spent a short while as a real estate broker for Hartz Mountain in Secaucus, New Jersey, and as the manager of a Greenwich Village auto body shop. He worked in various construction jobs and, then, on the strength of that experience, developed as an independent carpenter, going on to run his own small contracting firm.

He managed to save enough money through these enterprises to purchase a three-story frame house in the Forest Hill neighborhood of Newark—a quiet, elegant, old community of historic homes a mile north of downtown, and just a twenty-minute train ride from Manhattan. His new home bore the moniker "Madame Jeritza's Mansion."

DR. WELLS EAGLETON MARRIED FLORENCE PESHINE RIGGS ON May 27, 1913. For Wells, a man in his fifties, this was his first marriage. Florence was a widow with two sons from her previous marriage. She was a leader in the women's suffrage movement and an advocate for women's higher education. She was one of the first women to serve as a Trustee for Rutgers University. Dr. Eagleton was a prominent physician in New Jersey. He was the first doctor to complete an internship at the Newark Charitable Eye and Ear Infirmary. He continued to provide his professional services at the clinic until his death. He was chief of head surgery at Camp Dix during World War I and served as trustee for the State Commission for the Blind, the Newark Museum and the Newark Council of Social Agencies. He also supported his wife's passions—the pursuit of women's suffrage and world peace.

Florence owned a piece of land at 212 Elwood in the Forest Hill section of Newark. The development of this fifty-six-block community began in the 1870s and continued into the 1920s. The prime section of the neighborhood, on the Ballantine Parkway overlooking the New York skyline, housed the wealthiest families of the time in grand estates of brick and stone, complete with elaborate stained glass, embossed ceilings and embellished masonry. The creation before the turn of the century of Branch Brook Park—the first county park in the nation—enhanced the area's natural beauty and established its separate identity. Frederick Law Olmsted, who laid out New York's Central Park, designed this oasis and filled it with cherry trees. The springtime display of blossoms rivaled that of Washington, D.C., in its profusion and fragrance.

In the year of their marriage, the Eagletons built a two-and-a-half-story Colonial Revival home on the plot. Doric columns supported the portico and side porch of the clapboard-clad house. A hipped roof with dormers and leaded windows added to the home's gracious exterior. Their dwelling sat in majestic splendor with its one-story carriage house on a small hill, looking down on its neighbors. It was one of the showcases of the less prestigious area of Forest Hill. In addition to Wells and Florence, Florence's son Stafford and two live-in servants resided in the house.

Dr. Eagleton passed away in 1946. Florence remained at the home until her death in 1954. She donated more than one million dollars to establish the Wells Phillips Eagleton and Florence Peshine Eagleton Foundation—now known as the Institute of Politics—at Rutgers University.

On September 21, 1954, the estate sold the property—consisting of a main house, a guest house and a carriage house—to New Jersey umbrella manufacturer Irving Seery, the third husband of the much-lauded Madame Maria Jeritza, for $12,700. They had married six years earlier in Manhattan when Maria was 60 and Irving was 57 years old.

Madame Jeritza, also known as Baroness von Popper, a legacy from her first marriage to Baron Leopold von Popper, earned her fame as an internationally renowned soprano—the golden girl of opera's golden age. Born in Brunn, Austria, in 1887, she debuted on stage with the Vienna Royal Opera in 1912 by special invitation of Emperor

Franz Josef. She exploded into stardom in the States in 1921 as a prima donna with the Metropolitan Opera.

Tall, blonde and with a commanding presence and powerful voice, she added fire and color to every role. Madame Jeritza's reputation soared after her performance as Floria Tosca, her stately but sinister characterization of Violetta and her slightly over-the-top portrayal of Minnie in the 1929 revival of Puccini's *The Girl of the Golden West*. She was credited with receiving the largest ovation ever in the Metropolitan's history after singing the second-act aria of Tosca while prostrate on the floor. She performed with the Metropolitan Opera for the last time in 1932. Many of the tenors and other sopranos were relieved to see her go. The tempestuous diva had feuded with them constantly.

She continued to tour Europe and the United States for years. In 1935, she returned to Vienna for a performance. Normally, a visit from Jeritza was a time of national celebration, crowds mobbing the stage door whenever she sang in her home country. This time, however, she was greeted by public chastisement in the Catholic press. They disapproved of her Arkansas divorce from von Popper and her second marriage to Hollywood producer Winfield Richard Sheehan.

In the face of this criticism, Jeritza refused to sing. The Austrian government, seeing Jeritza as a national treasure, stepped in to broker a peace between the diva and her public. In an elaborate ceremony, they awarded her the Order of the Knighthood. Mollified, Jeritza sang for her countrymen.

In addition to the scandal of divorce and rumors of multiple torrid romances with composers and others, Jeritza had an additional claim to fame. In 1937, she and her second husband transported the first Lipizzaner horses—two stallions and two mares—from Austria to America for a movie based on Felix Salten's book, *Florian*. The couple later divorced—making room for husband number three.

To fill that role, Maria chose umbrella man Irving Seery, who purchased the Newark mansion for his bride. Irving and Maria undertook immediate changes to the property. Inside the home, they added a theater, creating a stage where Madame Jeritza could entertain her friends with her glorious voice. A more dramatic alteration came to the home with the erection of a fence to encircle the property. A five-foot-high concrete barrier topped with a ten-foot wrought-iron fence robbed the elegant structure of its openness and gave it a forbidding, almost ominous, look.

At Christmas time, though, it was the brightest spot in Forest Hill. The couple filled the property with lights and Christmas decorations. On foot and by car, families made the pilgrimage to Madame Jeritza's home, filling children with delight. Many homes had holiday pictures of their families posed in front of the elaborate mansion's display.

In 1967, they built a clumsy second-story addition on the carriage house, giving it the gawky look of a teenager in the midst of a growth spurt. Jeritza, wrapped in mink coats and adorned with her trademark diamond-studded sunglasses, filled the mansion with opera music until she passed away in July 1982 at the age of 94. She was laid to rest in the Seery family plot at Holy Cross Cemetery in North Arlington, New Jersey. As she lay in peace, her well-loved Newark mansion lay dormant for a few months—begging for the attention and maintenance that Jeritza, in her advanced age, had neglected for years.

John Caprio had no plans to return to Newark after his graduation from Arts High School years earlier. Nonetheless, when the director of music for the Roman Catholic Archdiocese of New York heard that Madame Jeritza's mansion was on the market, he had to see it.

The asking price was $250,000. The gloomy ambiance and shabby exterior put off many prospective buyers. John, on the other hand, saw beneath the run-down condition to the splendid, sound bones of the structure. The disinterest of others was a godsend for John. He and Robert Tornquist purchased the home in March of 1983 for a song. They paid less than half the listed price.

They made a tidy profit on September 29, 1986, when Dean purchased the home for $170,000. His mother and grandmother helped with the down payment, and his mother co-signed the loan. At that time, the gentrification of the neighborhood was still more a concept than a reality. Many of the homes begged for rejuvenation—or a simple demolition to put them out of their misery.

But Dean saw beyond the dreary façade of some of the homes around his. He envisioned a community graced by tall old trees, mature landscaping and stately homes. He knew Forest Hill was on the verge of reclaiming its lost glory, and he wanted to play a role in the neighborhood's beautification.

When he bought the house, he gained the services of Elizabeth, a Hungarian housekeeper in her sixties. Elizabeth began cleaning the home when Madame Jeritza established residence there three decades ago. She quickly grew fond—and very protective—of Dean, whom she treated like a son.

By day, Dean labored hard in the construction business, but on nights and weekends, he donned the persona of Lord of the manor. He was an instant magnet for the young teenaged girls in the neighborhood. They gathered in each others' second-story bedrooms, following his every move from the windows. He epitomized glamour in their eyes.

On New Year's Eve, 1987, a bevy of 15- and 16-year-old girls gathered in Tara Franks' second-floor bedroom.

They were at that awkward age—too young to celebrate the night at parties where champagne ruled over the festivities, and too old to go to bed and pretend it was just any old night of the year.

They sat on the bed and on the floor with bowls of popcorn, plates of cookies and all the soda they could drink, talking about boys, school and hopes about what the new year would bring. One girl served as look-out, eyes trained on Dean's house as she reported the arrival of each new person to the mansion.

"A limousine—a limousine just pulled up," the look-out squealed.

All the girls rushed to the windows. Noses pressed to the glass as they sighed into each other's ears. In moments their vigilance was rewarded with the sight they'd anticipated—Dean emerged from the house and headed down the sidewalk. He was surrounded by an entourage of men, but the girls only had eyes for him. In a tuxedo with a formal overcoat and a flash of white scarf around his neck, he was the stuff of dreams.

They watched in paralyzed delight as each man slid into the luxurious car. They did not move their eyes from the sight until the vehicle glided away from the curb, down the street and out of sight.

The girls had no idea that Dean was gay, but even if they had, it might not have mattered. He was exquisite eye candy. They loved to look at him and fantasize about the future.

When Halloween rolled around, Dean enchanted younger children in the neighborhood, too. Groups of Forest Hill's kids, bedecked in costumes ranging from the scary to the sublime, gathered by the wrought-iron gate at 212 Elwood. They gazed up at the spooky old house and set their imaginations free. They peered into the shadows, conjuring up visions of ghosts, witches and monsters.

They crept up the steps to the sidewalk, relishing the terror they felt as only children could—with the safety of knowing there was really nothing to fear.

They walked up to the porch and clustered near the door. After whispered exhortations and exchanged elbow jabs, one brave soul reached up, pressed the doorbell and jumped back into the comfort of the pack.

They gasped as the large front door flung open, and squealed at the first sight of the stuff of nightmares—Count Dracula. In a flowing black velvet cape, with piercing fangs, bloody lips and a sinister laugh, Dean Faiello acted the role to perfection, thrilling the neighborhood kids as he dropped treats into each sack. The giggles of the fleeing trick-or-treaters echoed in the trees as they bolted down the sidewalk and back to the street, heading out to claim their plunder from the next house in their path.

Dean charmed his adult neighbors as well. He was polite, pleasant, and always knew the right thing to say. He participated in block yard sales and community social events.

One afternoon, Dean sat on the front porch of his neighbor Leticia Franks' house sipping tea, chatting and watching the world go by. On the side of her house opposite Dean's place was one of the rattiest homes in the neighborhood—an affront to others whose work on their historic homes revitalized block after block.

Someone emerged from the home and stared at the two as they sat on the porch. Leticia's nose crinkled in distaste and disapproval. "They drive me crazy," she said. "They stare over at me whenever I sit on the porch like I was a storefront display set up for their enjoyment, or a caged animal performing for their amusement. And I hate having a view of that ramshackle place day after day."

"They are rude and that place is an eyesore," Dean sympathized.

"I wish I had something to block that side of the porch without blocking the breeze so I could sit on my porch in peace."

"No problem. I'll take care of that for you," Dean said, patting the back of her hand.

"You will?"

"Sure. Don't worry about it anymore."

Leticia eyed him as he finished his tea. When he excused himself, he went down her walk and through his back gate. She watched him, hopeful that he was serious, but fearful that he was only making polite conversation with no intention of following through on his promise. *People can be so phony*, she thought.

She was delighted a couple of days later to discover that her skepticism was totally unfounded. Two guys arrived on the scene with a sheet of lattice. They installed it on the far end of her porch, blocking the full view of the dreary structure next door and returning to her a measure of privacy. Dean had a new friend for life—or so it seemed at the time.

IF DEAN'S LIFE HAD REVOLVED AROUND HIS NEIGHBORLY INteractions, it would have been a lot brighter for him. But the dark side of his lifestyle—the frenetic social swirl of a hyper-attractive gay man in Manhattan—overtook him. Dean fell under the seductive spell of excessive alcohol consumption, cocaine use and parties with no end. Then, he stepped onto the path that led to his destruction. Pretty boy Dean abandoned construction work to make the world of beauty his occupation of choice.

CHAPTER EIGHT

IT STARTED INNOCENTLY ENOUGH. IN 1988, DEAN WALKED down Christopher Street in Greenwich Village and on impulse stepped inside The Beach, an oasis of white—walls, floors, chairs, table and uniforms—to Dean, it seemed like a beacon of purity in the midst of a strip of garish debauchery. He felt awkward and unsophisticated as he stepped up to the service counter. On the other side, Dean saw Michael Hart in a white tank top, "a blond Adonis with piercing sapphire blue eyes and a smile that could light up a midnight sky."

Michael was a savvy businessman who built a personal care salon with a sexy advertising campaign and long hours of hard work. He normally put in 16-hour days and ate his breakfast and lunch while he worked. He closed only twice a year: on Christmas, and on the day of the Gay Pride Parade, because the mob outside his door made it impossible for employees or customers to gain access to his business. Because of his success, Michael had a constant need for contracting work and hired Dean to do renovations for his new business. Soon, Michael and Dean were an item.

Dean abandoned his licentious lifestyle of serial boyfriends and made a commitment of exclusivity with

Michael. They split their time between Michael's apartment in Manhattan and Dean's house in Newark.

Michael, a reformed drug dealer, provided the discipline Dean needed. He didn't allow Dean the addict's refuge of denial. Michael made Dean face up to his addiction and enter a drug and alcohol rehabilitation program. He poured all the liquor in Dean's home down the drain to eliminate the temptation that can overwhelm a recovering addict. He made sure Dean attended AA meetings every few days without fail. Now Dean got high taking in Broadway shows and dining at good restaurants with his partner.

For Michael as well as for Dean's other gay friends, going out in public with Dean was a heady experience that bordered on the bizarre. He was an obvious focal point, attracting attention no matter where he was. People stared at him when he entered the theater. They couldn't take their eyes off of him when he sat in a restaurant. Women dropped phone numbers on him with hope twinkling in their eyes. Gay men approached him with the subtlety of mating sharks. Eating at an outdoor café was out of the question—the endless disruptions made it impossible to concentrate on a meal. Inside, at least, the audience was limited.

At times, Dean saw the reaction of those around him as a curse. He grew suspicious of people's motives and hidden agendas. He wanted to be accepted as himself—for his contribution—not just because of his façade. Some acquaintances said that he expressed a yearning to be one of the Gay 500, an informal A-list clique of wealthy gay men in Manhattan from a diverse range of professions. Dean was bound to be frustrated in the desire. The Gay 500 was just another urban legend in a city that gives birth to myths quicker that it can debunk them.

Dean found a few refreshing friendships with those who had no desire to bed him, but simply enjoyed his company. They were the rare people in Dean's life who found him a great listener and entertaining conversationalist—the men and women who shared his curiosity about life and everything in it. Michael was a newer and even more refreshing experience for Dean—a sexual partner whose interest was deeper and more genuine than that of simple lustful infatuation.

Michael noticed that Dean was unhappy in the construction field and encouraged him to attend electrolysis school.

Dean received his CPE—Certified Professional Electrologist—status from the American Electrology Association in 1993. At first, he worked two days a week at The Beach and continued with his carpentry work. Two days expanded to four, then, in no time, he was booked solid—six days a week—at $100 an hour. He had a large and loyal following who recognized and appreciated that Dean loved his work. He enjoyed taking care of his clients, nurturing them and making them happy.

Nonetheless, working at The Beach caused a lot of stress in Dean's life. Though his relationship with Michael continued to flourish, his interactions with his fellow employees were strained. Dean's good looks stirred up jealousies and his status as more-than-just-another-employee generated resentment. His friends said The Beach was a "den of vicious queens." Dean never felt he fit in there—but he stayed to work with Michael.

Dean then discovered the new technology of laser hair removal. He took classes to learn how to use the strange wand-like instrument. He learned how to sear individual hairs down to their roots. He used his own body to practice his technique. In time, he removed every strand of hair from his torso and his limbs, with the exception of his lower left leg. He left that hair growing in anticipation of new technological advances that would require future personal experimentation.

Dean's world teetered when Michael developed full-blown AIDS. Both men had known they were HIV positive, but now the reality of that diagnosis hit hard. A feeling of fatalism grew in Dean—the sense that there were no limits, because he might not be around long enough to face the consequences of any of his actions. "There is no greater feeling of emptiness than the void that envelops you as you sit alone in a hospital room watching your lover become more emaciated by the hour, listening to the cavernous echo of silence punctuated by the labored breathing of a once-healthy and formerly-stunning example of male beauty." Dean sat by Michael's side as he suffered through toxoplasmosis, cytomegalovirus and pneumocystis. "There is nothing like watching a life slip away while sitting on a hospital chair to give you a feeling of helplessness and insignificance."

Dying of AIDS was a lonely path for a gay man. The sufferer was often discarded by family and friends and left to die alone. In other cases the family stepped in and pushed what they perceived as bad influences out of the sick loved one's life. Those men lost contact with many who could have brightened their final days.

The break-up of Michael and Dean's relationship was an ugly chapter in Dean's life. Many believed Dean turned his back on Michael when his lover became ill. He received a lot of criticism for abandoning Michael in his hour of need. Other people who knew the couple said that the truth was far more complicated: that Michael's family swooped in from Jacksonville, Florida, and Dean was out of the picture. Michael's parents came by the Newark house to claim their son's belongings. Housekeeper Elizabeth took an instant dislike to them—they struck her as uppity, bossy and greedy. She eyeballed them the whole time they were in the house, with all the tethered suspicion of a leashed guard dog. She feared that without her constant vigilance, they'd walk out with everything of value in the home.

Michael, vulnerable and dependent in his illness, could do nothing to change the sequence of events. He moved back to Florida with his family, leaving Dean in New York.

Dean summed up the situation simply: "As with many patients with terminal illness, Michael got very angry at his disease. Eventually, he turned his anger toward me, as I was nearest to him. He was frightened and so was I."

At least Michael was not alone. His family gathered round and supported him in his final days. Michael died in the Sunshine State in November 1995.

WITHOUT MICHAEL AT THE SPA TO PROTECT HIM, THE NASTIness toward Dean at The Beach escalated. With no one holding the reins on his substance abuse—and with the increased awareness of his own mortality looming over every moment of his day—Dean renewed his drug use, at first with the occasional use of microdots and ecstasy. Then it flew out of control as the occasional became frequent, and his heavy consumption of alcohol and cocaine resumed.

CHAPTER NINE

JASON OPSAHL ENTERED DEAN'S LIFE IN 1995. JASON, A talented Broadway performer, was born to Robert and Muriel Opsahl in Savannah, Georgia, on December 9, 1962. He was their fourth child. Jason had three older brothers: Robert, Bart and Craig.

Dad was in the Air Force, and the family moved around with his changes in orders. They lived in California, Michigan and Minnesota before settling down in Orlando when Jason was still a small child. He made his first entrance on stage in a production of *Oliver!* at an area educational institution, Rollins College. Jason was just 8 years old. That experience set him on an exciting career path.

Through high school, he sang, danced and acted in regional theater as well as at Orlando-area theme parks.

Jason majored in Theatre Arts at Rollins College in the nearby town of Winter Park on the shores of Lake Virginia—it was the oldest recognized college in Florida. He graduated in 1984 and headed to New York City and the bright lights of Broadway in 1986.

For five and a half years, Jason took whatever roles he could get—even playing the part of Sperm No. 2 in *The Fertilization Opera*, an off-Broadway show.

But shortly thereafter, doubting his ability to succeed, Jason made a trip to Orlando for the ten-year reunion of his Boone High School class. While there, he heard about auditions for Tommy Tune's new show. He tried out—and then waited . . . and waited. Finally, in early December— just days before his birthday—he got the news. He was cast as a wrangler in *The Will Rogers Follies* starring David Carradine.

On the first day of rehearsal, Jason stopped at a nearby deli. As he left, Jerry Mitchell, another dancer and aspiring choreographer, was on his way into the shop to pick up some lunch. Jerry had never seen Jason before, but wondered if the young man coming out of the deli was in the show, because he thought the tall blonde had the attractiveness, magnetism and presence of a Broadway star. When they two men met on the stage after lunch, they smiled in recognition.

Jerry sat beside Jason in the dressing room. Soon, Jerry knew he'd met a man with whom he could be completely honest. He discovered that he felt comfortable talking to Jason about their lives, their dreams, their fears—things Jerry never could share with anyone else. It was this quality in Jason that formed the bedrock of his later relationship with Dean Faiello.

With his Broadway debut on May 1, 1991, Jason and his angelic high tenor voice won the hearts of New York's theater crowd. In the first act, Jerry Mitchell played the role of the Indian of the Dawn. To say his costume left him half-naked would exaggerate the amount of clothing he wore. "Besides the headdress and bells, not much else covered my body," Jerry said. His scanty attire before the curtain rose was a constant source of humor for the cast and crew, who gave him a lot of light-hearted ribbing. One day, Jason said, "You ought to wear that to dance at Splash"—a gay bar on West 17th Street between Broadway and the Avenue of the Americas. "You could raise a lot of money for Broadway Cares," a joint effort between the Producers Group and the Council of Actors' Equity Association to fund AIDS, HIV and HIV-related health issues.

That off-hand comment helped give birth to a charitable effort that remained dear to Jason's heart all of his life. In 1991, Jerry, Jason and six other dancers put on the first one-night benefit event performance of *Broadway Bares* at Splash. Their entertaining but raucous routines raised $8,000 for the charity, now known as Broadway Cares/Equity Fights AIDS. In a year when the theater world lost many lives to AIDS, the cause was near and dear to many hearts.

Broadway Bares continued as an annual fundraiser along with two other theater-oriented yearly events: the Gypsy of the Year award and the Easter Bonnet Competition. Jason devoted his talents to all of these money-raising opportunities for the organization. In the second year, they added women to the *Broadway Bares* show and the take for charity escalated.

Jason worked every year with the production and performance crew for twelve annual shows in a row, functioning either as emcee or as caller for the go-go dancing rotation at the finale of each performance—or both. Each year, the theme of the production changed and a new theme song was written. In years when the music suited Jason's voice, he would take on the responsibility of singing as well.

In Jason's final year with *Broadway Bares* on June 16, 2002, at the Comic Strip on Second Avenue, the dedicated performers brought in $400,000 for BC/EFA. His active participation in this show, combined with his zest for life, his never-ending words of encouragement to his fellow performers, and his willingness to always put others before himself earned Jason the nickname of "the mayor of Broadway." His cachet tantalized Dean, who yearned to bask in Jason's glory.

WHEN JASON AND DEAN MET IN 1995, JASON WAS PERFORMING on Broadway in a new show, Tommy Tune's revival production of *Grease*. He had not planned or prepared for his audition. Often at try-outs, he sang "When You Wish Upon a Star," weaving a web of wonder around all who listened. "He made you believe every word, because he seemed to believe it. He made you feel like a child again," Jerry Mitchell said. "The belief shone from his eyes. He was the real Peter Pan—the goodness of a child in the package of a man."

At this audition, though, he performed a song he'd never sung before and danced a routine he hardly knew. He didn't expect to hear back from director Jeff Calhoun. But he did—the biggest surprise of all was learning he landed a principal role: Kenickie, the leader of the pack at Rydell High and the romantic interest of Betty Rizzo, the head of the girl gang, the Pink Ladies, played by Rosie O'Donnell. It was the start of a beautiful friendship.

It also gave Jason entrée into a high-flying social world—occasions that crawled with a plethora of Hollywood stars. Dean finagled an introduction to Jason through a mutual friend. Jason was captivated by Dean's good looks and charm. Jason saw the good in everyone—and initially, overlooked every flaw. He escorted Dean to events. It was a new experience for Dean and he loved the glamour of it.

Jason and Dean took trips to Orlando to meet Jason's parents and brothers. The family, in turn, visited the couple in New York. At one point in their relationship, Jason needed a loan. Dean obliged. In exchange for loaning Jason a couple thousand dollars, Jason assigned Dean as beneficiary of his Actors Guild pension. At the time, the fund's value was roughly equivalent to the amount of Dean's loan. Dean had no idea that in a matter of years, the fund would grow many times over—and prove to be a heated battleground.

In early January 1996, Jason was in the cast of *Andrew Lloyd Webber: Music of the Night*, a revival of the original 1989 show. On opening night at the Tupperware Convention Center in Osceola County, Florida, leading man Colm Wilkinson's throat infection kept him off the stage. Jason stepped into the role, and his flawless, versatile singing voice earned him a cheering ovation from his hometown crowd.

During the show's run, they picked up sultry-voiced Melissa Manchester as the star. Melissa, Jason and Julie Patton opened the curtain in Houston, Texas, with a performance of "As If We Never Said Goodbye" from *Sunset Boulevard*. Critics praised Jason for his performance in the opening number as well as his songs from *Cats* and *Phantom of the Opera*.

Jason's schedule of on-the-road performances strained his relationship with Dean. Always sexually active, Dean's committment to a long-distance relationship was tenuous, at best.

In 1997, while rehearsing for *Harmony*, a Barry Manilow musical, fate forced Jason's career into an unexpected hiatus. In September, without warning, he went into seizures. After emergency surgery to remove a tumor, Jason received a diagnosis of anaplastic astrocytoma level 3, an aggressive form of brain cancer. The doctor said he only had only six months to live.

Jason faced astronomical medical bills. Rosie O'Donnell stepped forward and helped with that expense. She also provided airfare for Jason to fly back and visit his family.

Dean never made a vow to stick by his partner in sickness and in health. But even if he had, it was not an oath that Dean was equipped to keep.

Three weeks later, Jason returned to Orlando, Florida. His brother Bart smiled as he watched his younger sibling jumping on the trampoline in his backyard, defying the odds. After a year with his family, Jason's recovery from brain surgery appeared complete. He hit the boards on Broadway again, exhibiting the same enthusiasm and intense energy he possessed before his medical crisis. If anything, his spirits were even higher than before. He approached each day thankful to be alive and appreciative that he was able to work again. The final curtain closed, however, on his relationship with Dean.

CHAPTER TEN

AROUND THE SAME TIME HE HOOKED UP WITH JASON, DEAN made another change in his life. He paid a visit to the Medical Health Care group and spoke with Dr. Laurie Polis. He told her, "I want to move my practice to a medical setting."

Laurie was born on December 18, 1956, in Mount Vernon, New York. In 1978, she graduated with a Bachelor of Science Degree and an RN from the State University of New York in Buffalo. She received her medical degree from the Mount Sinai School of Medicine in 1983, earning honors in medicine, psychiatry and pediatrics. She served her internship at the Lenox Hill Hospital of New York and completed her residency in Dermatology and Dermatologic Surgery at the Albert Einstein College of Medicine of Yeshiva University, practicing at their affiliated Montefiore Medical Center in the Bronx.

Along the way, she received certification from the Diplomat National Board of Medical Examiners and the American Board of Dermatology. The state of New York awarded her with licenses to practice medicine, nursing and acupuncture.

She retained academic positions as well. She taught at various dermatology departments, working as an adjunct clinic instructor at the Mount Sinai School of Medicine, as a clinical instructor at Beth Israel Medical Center and as an Assistant Professor at the Albert Einstein College of Medicine.

Laurie married an obstetrician–gynecologist and they had twin girls in 1991. In that same year, Laurie opened the Medical Health Care Group on Crosby Street in SoHo, serving as Administrative and Dermatology Director.

Highly regarded by her peers, she presented the keynote address at numerous medical meetings and conferences. She racked up an impressive number of publication credits and television interviews as an expert in dermatologic problems and treatments.

When Dean came calling, Dr. Polis was affiliated with four hospitals and a consultant for a long list of corporations including Pond's, Gillette, Clearasil and Novartis Pharmaceuticals. She took her continuing professional education seriously. The list of post-doc courses she had mastered grew with each passing year.

She recognized that Dean possessed an innate knack for a soothing bedside manner. She was impressed with his desire to learn and aware that his good looks were an asset in the beauty business.

Dean and Laurie reached an agreement and Dean left the stifling environment at The Beach. Dean performed electrolysis in her facility as an independent contractor. He set his own hours, used his own equipment and saw his own group of clients. Polis referred patients in need of electrolysis to Dean, and Dean referred clients who needed a dermatologist to Dr. Polis.

Observing Dean, she was pleased with the arrangement. He practiced prudent aseptic techniques and was fastidious about his personal appearance, the condition of the treatment room and the care of any patients she referred to him. She witnessed no signs of duplicity—no indication that he was anything less than a consummate professional.

At the time Dean joined the group, the world of dermatology was just beginning to welcome laser technology into its treatment regimen. Trained as a laser surgeon, Dr. Polis introduced the technology to her patients. Dean expressed an interest in observing and learning about the technique. He had some experience with the early technology of laser but none with the state-of-the-art laser machines used in Laurie's practice.

"If I know about it, I will know when to refer a client to you for laser instead of performing electrolysis," he said.

Dr. Polis agreed as long as he informed the patients in advance and obtained their consent. It was not an unusual request in her facility. Often medical students, residents, other doctors and staff sat in on her procedures.

Dean referred several patients to Dr. Polis for laser work and was on hand with them from beginning to end. He was a helpful asset to the doctor. He moved patients in and out of the treatment room and jotted down notes. His inquisitive and enthusiastic manner made his presence a pleasure.

Dean actively participated in other areas at the center. He fixed equipment all over the office. He attended the center's marketing meetings and contributed valuable input.

He built a strong clientele at the SoHo facility that included some straight women, but was dominated by gay men who wanted electrolysis or laser to look good on the beach at Fire Island, and transsexuals who were mainly interested in removing the hair from their faces.

Unbeknownst to Dr. Polis, Dean discovered the highly addictive Stadol NS, an opiate nasal spray, while he worked at her facility. The active ingredient, butorphanol, induced a morphine-like state of calm. In no time, he was hooked.

After working there for several months, Dean resigned. "I am dying of AIDS," he said. "I'm going to move to Florida to spend the rest of my days with my parents down there."

Dr. Polis and the rest of the doctors and staff at the center were shocked. They knew Dean was gay. They were aware of the horrible loss of life that streaked through the homosexual community in New York. But Dean? He looked fit and strong—the epitome of good health.

They were saddened by the news. They all liked him and enjoyed working with him. They knew they would miss him and grieve over his death at such a young age. They threw a farewell party giving gifts and best wishes to Dean as they sent him on his way. It was hard to lose a co-worker to the threat of an untimely death.

DEAN WAS HIV POSITIVE—BUT DYING OF AIDS? HARDLY. Parents in Florida? Not exactly. He stole Michael Hart's story and claimed it as his own. He decided to set up his own business and steal patients for both electrolysis and laser. He found it easy to seduce the trannies over to his camp. Eradicating facial hair on someone with a full beard took many long sessions. Each zap with the laser was like a slap. Each jolt of electrolysis felt like a stab. Individually, they were not too bad, but the repetition made it nearly unbearable. He promised prospective clients a reduced rate and the use of lidocaine to numb the area under treatment. To seal the deal, he bad-mouthed Dr. Polis to drive them to his door.

Dani Samuelson, a transsexual with long dark hair, a slim body and a cute face, first saw Dean at Dr. Polis' clinic on April 20, 1996. He started out treating her and others after hours in Dr. Polis' office. Dani saw him twice in May and once in August at the SoHo location. Before the end of the year, he'd left the SoHo clinic and started SkinOvations—a name suggested by Dani—at a dentist's office on 23rd Street.

THE FIRST DAY SHE ENTERED HIS NEW OFFICE, DANI WAS NERvous, not knowing what to expect of Dean's new facility. A receptionist with a French accent greeted her as she opened the door and invited her to take a seat.

Dani breathed in deep and exhaled some of her building apprehension. Before each treatment to remove the dark facial hair, the same consuming sense of dread settled on her stomach, making her queasy. She hated the pain.

Dean, however, told her he would inject the area with lidocaine. He promised she wouldn't feel a thing during the procedure. Dani knew that without the pain, she could sit through a longer session—and that meant fewer sessions before the ordeal was complete.

The expense would be less, too. Dean offered her a discounted rate when he lured her from the SoHo clinic. Everything about gender transformation was so expensive. Like Dean's other tranny clients, she appreciated his consideration of her economic limitations. Her friend, Laura Lorne, had told her about sessions with Dean where the hair removal procedure ran over the allotted time, but Dean didn't charge extra.

Dani did wonder if it was legal for Dean to administer the lidocaine injections, but decided she didn't care. Eliminating her big moustache was painful—the upper lip was one of the most sensitive parts of the body. This wasn't a medical procedure, she thought. It was just a beauty treatment like a haircut or massage.

Dani's reverie ended when she heard her name called out. She followed her escort down the hall to the treatment room. As she waited for Dean, she began to relax in the quiet, peaceful environment surrounding her—a welcome change from other venues. No raised voices. No boisterous people.

Dean entered the room in a crisp, white, knee-length jacket, looking every bit a competent, knowledgeable practitioner. On his hand, a huge diamond ring sparkled—a legacy from his grandfather Carmine Faiello. He flashed a winning smile and welcomed Dani with his soft-spoken voice.

The anxiety that coursed through Dani up to this moment was released from her pores and evaporated into nothing. As a rule, Dani felt uncomfortable around gay men—always on guard for a put-down. Dean, however, was different from most—at least in the office environment. She thought he was smarmy in what she referred to as a stereotypical gay guy way, but he was gentle, understanding about trannies' specific needs and never treated her like an outcast.

Dean apologized for the sting of the needle and the burn of the anesthetic. In moments, the unpleasant sensations were gone as numbness crept over Dani's skin. Dean got to work with his laser, zapping unwanted hair follicles. Dani made it through a full hour of treatment with nothing more than minor discomfort. Very pleased with the day's experience, she set her next appointment before leaving the building.

A POSITIVE, TENSION-FREE INTERACTION BETWEEN A TRANNY and a gay man was a rare moment for someone like Dani. Although it's politically correct to speak of the GLBT—gay, lesbian, bisexual, transgender—community, in reality, trannies found exclusion all around.

Most gay activists and the organizations they support adopt an inclusive attitude toward transsexuals and transgender individuals. A recent survey indicates that two-thirds of homosexuals favor inclusion. In the remaining third, insecurity and lack of enlightenment are likely compounded by the image of the flamboyant drag queen—many of whom are in fact heterosexuals who cross-dress for fun or a paycheck. Their over-the-top behavior creates a perception that has led to discrimination by gay men toward trannies that is real, even if not universal. However, every instance of discrimination felt all-encompassing to the victim, and Dani was keenly aware of each slight.

From her viewpoint, gay men keep transsexuals at arm's length because of their fear of negative repercussions in public perception. They believe gays worry that inclusion of trannies at their social events would make them appear more effeminate and therefore, less acceptable to straight society.

Dani felt that a more central issue of public perception for gay men resulted from the behavior of the few. Gay Pride parades that feature mock or actual displays of sexual acts are offensive to Middle America—just as the same overt acting out by heterosexuals offends sensibilities. If the straight population could simply associate the sexual excess seen in gay pride parades with that of similar exhibitions by male–female couples in New York's Puerto Rican parade, or the breast-flashing of women for beads in New Orleans during Mardi Gras, rather than regarding them as a hallmark of homosexuality, it would go far in minimizing strife between the two groups. That time, however, had not yet arrived for Dani and other transsexuals, who'd come to expect ostracism from straights and gays alike. When a man like Dean demonstrated no bias, it naturally came as a surprise.

Lesbian society was no bastion of enlightenment, either. Dani rarely found acceptance there. The women who came out in the sixties and seventies, in particular, had a strong belief in their credentials as lesbian women. They saw trannies as faux-women—men in disguise. They felt these people had grown up with the advantages of male privilege and were now co-opting everything women worked so hard to achieve, an assessment that denied the reality of life for Dani.

Complicating the issue was the fact that many transsexuals did not have the money or the medical prerequisites to complete the gender reassignment through surgery. Although living like women, they still were physically equipped as men.

The drama of this conflict hit a high point at the Michigan Womyn's Music Festival. The three-decades-old annual event covers 650 acres in rural Michigan each August. Thousands of lesbians gather for music, workshops, film and more in an all-woman venue. In 1991, the festival organizers expelled Nancy Burkholder, a transwoman, from the festivities. After two years of trying to get the policies of the event changed, trannies formed Camp Trans a half-mile down the road. It evolved into an event in its own right. Nonetheless, for Dani, the exclusion by mainstream America remained painful.

A new attitude among younger lesbians may one day bring the policy to an end. Women in their twenties and thirties have embraced a concept of sexual fluidity and possess a greater willingness to allow individuals an open expression of identity. Dani dreamed of that day, but was pessimistic about its arrival in her lifetime.

CHAPTER ELEVEN

DANI SAMUELSON INTRODUCED HER FRIEND MURIEL FARINA to Dean Faiello. Muriel, a Cuban-American trained and certified in electrolysis, wanted to expand her knowledge about hair removal by learning laser techniques. The two struck a deal: Muriel would bring Dean clients who could benefit from laser hair removal, and Dean would treat them while teaching Muriel. The two of them would split the fees fifty–fifty. They started out practicing at the 23rd Street location.

Dean stayed at that office for a short time before moving his operations to the Lexington Professional Center, an Upper East Side medical complex at 133 East 73rd Street—less than a block from Park Avenue. His offices adjoined those of Dr. William Keavy.

Keavy, a highly regarded specialist in plastic and reconstructive surgery, wrote the necessary prescriptions for Dean's clients and provided the lidocaine for injections. It was puzzling that a professional of Keavy's stature would be taken in by Dean's façade and not question his credentials. Some doctors who enabled Dean's practice and addictions throughout the years turned their backs on common sense and ethics because of the sexual attraction they had for Faiello or out of a greedy willingness to accept fees for the questionable services they provided.

Whether either of these motivations drove Keavy—or if there was some other unknown compulsion at work—may never be known with any certainty.

Although not working in the same office, Keavy was the nominal medical director of SkinOvations and Dean was the chief laserist. Dean, the college drop-out, also claimed on line to have a master's degree in engineering from RPI.

Meanwhile, Muriel kept up her business in an independent office space, but was working at Dean's two days a week for three hours at a time. She noticed that a great number of his clients were gay men who had or were having a sexual relationship with Dean.

She was concerned about the number of clients who ranted and raved in the front office about the ineffectiveness of their laser treatments. She recalled one man in particular who said, "I've given you five thousand dollars. You told me the hair would disappear."

Dean soothed him, as he did everyone with complaints, but Muriel grew increasingly uncomfortable. She didn't know where the fault lay—with Dean's operation of the equipment, the particular type of machine or that the technology proved far more effective on the lower half of the torso than it did on any areas above the waistline. Overall, the situation made her doubt whether it was wise to add laser services to her electrolysis business. She was still eager to learn more, but Dean was not as willing to teach her as he had been when they first met.

He did allow Muriel to practice using the laser on his lower back, but that was it. The rest of the time, Muriel took care of the electrology work that Dean did not want to do. When Muriel brought in her customers for laser hair removal, Dean would not instruct her as they had agreed. He simply did the work himself—and kept all the money, too. To Muriel, it seemed as if he were robbing her of clients and cheating her out of revenue.

Behind her back, Dean told Muriel's clients, "You do not want Muriel doing this. She is not ready yet." To Muriel's face, he said, "Well, I can't help it. Your clients just don't want to go to you anymore."

She knew Dean presented an excellent bedside manner. He was calm, patient, attractive and unpretentious; it did not surprise her that her clients found him likeable. Still, she and Dean had an agreement and Dean was not fulfilling his part of the bargain.

She listened to his lame excuses for a few weeks, then confronted him. "I don't want to believe that what you are doing is unethical. I want to assume there is a misunderstanding. There must be a reason you are not teaching me."

Dean, however, would not respond. He would not engage in any discussion or conversation about the issues between them. He just shut her out.

Muriel gave up, packed up her equipment and terminated the relationship. She got her laser education elsewhere.

WITH OR WITHOUT DR. KEAVY'S KNOWLEDGE, DEAN EXPANDED his services to include tattoo removal, benign pigmented lesion removal, vascular lesion removal and laser skin resurfacing, a procedure that destroys the top layer of the epidermis, allowing fresh, new skin to take its place.

Since New York was one of the few states that did not require a medical license to operate a laser, performing these procedures and giving lidocaine injections did not technically break the law—especially given the supposed oversight of Dr. Keavy. But Dean pushed closer and closer to the edge.

He claimed that he was certified in laser skin treatments, and he did in fact have certificates for every laser class he attended. But when he advertised that he was a member of the American Society for Laser Medicine &

Surgery, he crossed a line. The organization did not require its members to be physicians, but he alluded to his affiliation with it in a manner that made it sound like a claim of medical school education.

BY 1997, DEAN BEGAN PASSING HIMSELF OFF AS A DERMATOLO-gist. His ruse convinced enough people that when Linda Burke prepared to move from San Francisco to New York, her dermatologist on the West Coast recommended Dr. Dean Faiello.

The skies were gray on the winter morning that Linda approached Dean's office building for the first time to finish the hair removal she started in California. Vicious cold blanketed the city. She thought it quite odd that in the middle of the winter in Manhattan, her new doctor sported a golden tan. All the other dermatologists she knew tended to look pasty every month of the year, avoiding over-exposure to the rays that induced such a glow.

The tan, though, did add to Dean's exceptional good looks, as did the genetic endowment of glorious dark eyelashes, the man-made, tailored arch of his eyebrows and the symmetry of his tight, fresh beard. Dean gave off an air that said he was conscious of the perfection of his looks—much like the smug smirk on the face of a haughty cat after an intense session of meticulous grooming.

Dean, in a soft voice, explained the wonders of his state-of-the-art laser hair-removal machine. He told her that he used it on himself on a regular basis. *Like that isn't obvious*, she thought.

Linda laid back on the table for her treatment. She remained prone, trying to relax. "I'm going to apply the specialty healing lotion now," Dean told her.

Linda opened her eyes and saw Dean squeezing a thick liquid into his gloved hand. The label on the bottle read: "Vaseline Intensive Care Lotion." Bemused, she shut her eyes and felt the soothing coolness on her skin.

She assumed, based on her physician's referral, that Dean was a medical doctor. He never told her he was. She never thought to ask.

And she never thought about Dean Faiello again in the seven years that followed.

DURING LINDA BURKE'S TREATMENT SESSION, DEAN DID nothing illegal, immoral or unethical. But he was unquestionably committing illegal acts when he wrote prescriptions for Stadol and signed Dr. Laurie Polis' name. The drug, prescribed for migraine headaches, was hard to find on the streets, and Dean used as much as a bottle a day to feed his habit. When he started using Stadol, the bottles were $100 apiece; but as time went on, the price rose to $250 a pop, making it a rather costly addiction. Often, he used his American Express card to pay for his Stadol, creating a paper trail that investigators would eventually follow with ease.

When his clients got prescriptions for Stadol from their doctors, to relax them during laser procedures, Dean often pocketed the slightly used bottles while the customer was too dazed to notice. If one of them called about it after his head cleared, he found it easy to believe Dean's denial, and to suspect that he had lost it someplace else.

AFTER DEAN MOVED INTO HIS UPPER EAST SIDE OFFICE, DR. Polis was flipping through *New York* magazine. An ad for the opening of a new laser clinic and multi-specialty medical center caught her eye. The marketing angle replicated the one she used for her own business.

She looked closer, her curiosity transforming into surprise, then sinking in a queasy recognition of betrayal. The director and laserist listed in the ad for this new center was none other than Dean Faiello. He'd manipulated her sympathy with a tale of fatal illness and, under a cloak of deception, used her expertise to further his own business objectives.

She knew New York state did not require a medical license to operate a laser—not for hair removal. But Dean offered more. He described himself as a medical practitioner well versed in laser technology and willing to remove "ugly brown spots" and other lesions.

Dr. Polis was alarmed. *How could Dean know the difference between harmless benign solar lentigines and the deadly lentigo maligna melanomas?* She knew his lack of medical training put his clients at risk. From Dr. Polis' viewpoint, it was clear that Dean was practicing medicine without a license.

She went to her computer and logged on to the Internet, pulling up the website for Dean's business, SkinOvations. Once again, she faced a marketing message that mimicked her own. Now she knew why Dean was so eager and active in their marketing meetings.

The website claimed that SkinOvations had a number of medical practitioners on staff. Dr. Polis called the office number. From the woman at the front desk, she learned that the whole business consisted of the receptionist, Dean Faiello and a single treatment room with a laser machine.

Dr. Polis believed she had an ethical responsibility to take action when she observed someone posing a medical risk to public safety. Someone had to protect Dean's clients. She called the state department of education and got nowhere. She called the state health department, who told her that they could not take action until they had a consumer complaint about a violation of public health regulations.

She found no help at the police department, either.

"What crime is he committing if it's not illegal for him to run a laser?" they asked.

When she called the state attorney general's office, they referred her to District Attorney Robert Morganthau. His office referred her in turn to the assistant district attorney's office, but did not name any particular individual as a contact. She left repeated messages, but no one ever returned her calls.

She contacted the federal Drug Enforcement Agency, but they insisted it was not a drug problem and not in their jurisdiction. The Better Business Bureau claimed they could do nothing about his false advertising. The state Department of Consumer Affairs said it was a matter for the legal authorities. Unfortunately, they were unable to tell her *which* legal authority would be most likely to take action.

After exhausting every possible government organization that popped into her head—she made fifty-four phone calls before she lost count—Dr. Polis called *New York* magazine to complain. "We take money for advertising, label it as advertising, but we do not assume any responsibility for the content."

Dr. Polis brought up the issue at several dermatology meetings. The other physicians shared her concerns, but did not know who she could contact to stop Dean Faiello. One physician expressed interest in helping her in her quest—the director of the Laser & Skin Surgery Center of New York, Dr. Roy Geronemus.

He'd heard Dean Faiello's name before. Patients arrived in his office with scarring and permanent changes in skin pigmentation over the treated areas. Some received treatments in spas from uncertified practitioners. Some visited physicians who were not dermatologists or plastic surgeons—just doctors who got a laser, attended a crash weekend course and expanded their practice in pursuit of a quick buck. In one case, a model's career was cut short after an oral surgeon used a laser to remove a lesion on her face and left a large scar on her lip.

With increasing frequency, these scarred patients mentioned the name of Dr. Dean Faiello. The damage-causing treatments they received at his hands included hair removal, but also the removal of lesions and tattoos. Dr. Geronemus decided to check out Dr. Faiello and discovered that he did not possess a license to practice medicine in the state of New York.

Now he, too, was concerned about this fake doctor. "You must have training in the presenting problem as well as in the device being used," he said. "You have to have sufficient knowledge and education to exercise clinical judgment, because lasers interact with the skin in different ways, depending on a patient's age, skin type and skin color.

"Entrepreneurial types like Dean Faiello believe they can operate this machinery based on technical knowledge but without medical training. As a result, they're flying under the radar and hurting people."

Dr. Geronemus filed a complaint about Dean's unlicensed practice of medicine with the Office of Professional Discipline at the state department of education. Then he waited for them to do the right thing.

CHAPTER TWELVE

IN EARLY 1998, AFTER THE RELATIONSHIP BETWEEN DEAN and Jason fell apart, Dean partied one night at G, a Chelsea bar he'd frequented for years. It was the beginning of his relationship with event planner Greg Bach.

Greg's father was a cowboy and a rancher who went back to school and earned a degree in Chemical Engineering. He worked for an American-owned company that had transferred him, his wife and two children from the hot, nearly tropical environment of San Antonio, Texas, to Alberta, Canada. Two additional children were born to the Bach family before Greg came along on July 5, 1960. He grew up with two brothers and two sisters in Montreal.

At the age of four, he started training for competitive swimming, spending two to six hours in the water every day. At 14, he swam in his first international competition. When he turned 16, he made the national team. His events were the 100-meter and 200-meter breast stroke. He competed in the Pan American Games, Commonwealth Games and in the World Championships for four years as an internationally ranked swimmer.

While still competing, Greg moved to New York City—where he'd fantasized about living for most of his life. But he found the price tag for living in the city of his dreams too steep for a swimmer.

The discounted flights from New York to London were enticing, and the 20-year-old eventually decided to pack his bags and move to England. He found a job modeling in Europe. He remained on that side of the Atlantic for four years. The magical pull of New York tugged at his heart strings the whole time he was gone.

In 1984, he returned to Manhattan to study art and design. He attended the National Academy of Design and the School of Visual Arts. As he studied, he experimented with sculpture and discovered his medium—human figurative sculpting in sand. He rendered oversized figures on the beaches of Fire Island and East Hampton, photographing their demise as the tide rolled in and wiped them away. The end result was a poetic and allegoric series of shots depicting gradual destruction. He had no way of knowing that his art foreshadowed his life. As the sand returned to the sea, he couldn't know that one day he would watch a different force wipe away the life of a person dear to him—Dean Faiello.

Greg's sand-sculpting project brought him in contact with a major event designer who hired him as a freelancer to create huge bird sculptures out of moss, palms and orchids for an event at The Metropolitan Opera House. He hired Greg again to paint a backdrop for a boy's bar mitzvah celebration. That led to a full-time position in the company's floral department.

Greg enjoyed event work and saw the need for a business that could provide the same service on a smaller scale for more modest events. He stepped out on his own to fill that need. Through the New York City Business Solutions Center he found mentoring support and seminars that provided the information he needed to face critical business issues and increase his odds of success. Small businesses often come to an end because their owners are unaware of business taxes and other regulatory issues, or through a lack of proper planning. Greg availed himself of all the resources he could find to increase his likelihood of success.

His entrepreneurial effort was in its earliest stages when he first started dating Dean. That wasn't the first time, though, that Greg had noticed him. The two men had been in their early twenties when the initial encounter took place. Greg thought Dean was absolutely gorgeous. He was smitten at first sight.

After a few occasions in which both were at the same place at the same time, Greg finally got up the nerve to approach Dean. It took a lot of gumption for a quiet guy like Greg. It seemed a crowd of people engulfed Dean wherever he went. The first conversation was a flop. Greg felt awkward. Dean looked bored.

A couple of years after that fruitless encounter, Greg walked into a bar and spotted Dean sitting at a table by himself. He still nurtured an enormous crush on Dean and could not believe his luck.

The two men talked together for an hour and a half. Then, Dean gave Greg a ride home. As Greg left the car, the two exchanged phone numbers. To Greg's dismay, Dean never called.

A while later, Greg was at a friend's house watching a video of a birthday party on Fire Island. There was Dean. But he wasn't alone. He was with Michael Hart and it was obvious that the two men were involved in a relationship.

His heart sighed and Greg let go of his infatuation. Still, in the back of his mind he retained an image of Dean as his ideal. He wanted someone in his life with Dean's good looks and a house outside of the city. It would be a perfect arrangement—Greg's apartment in town and a getaway outside of Manhattan for when they wanted to escape the bustle.

The night that Dean and Greg both ended up at G, Greg

did not at first recognize Dean—a lot of time passed since the last time their paths crossed and they'd both aged a bit. Christopher Buczek offered to re-introduce Greg to Dean. As they approached, Christopher whispered, "Be sure to tell Dean you're an internationally ranked swimmer. Dean thinks swimmers are really sexy."

Greg and Dean spent hours together that evening. Greg parted from him in a state of enchantment. The next day, Dean sealed the deal—he sent Greg a dozen red roses.

A few nights later, when they were together again, Greg confessed, "I'm seeing a lawyer on Long Island."

"Oh, no problem," Dean flipped back, "I can handle the competition."

Greg never thought about that lawyer again. The new couple dated in earnest, enjoying nights at the theater, going to movies and dining at nice restaurants. Together they went to see Jason Opsahl perform in *The Full Monty* and *Broadway Bares*. They had a particularly good time at the Actors' Equity Show, a one-night benefit performance where actors put on an impromptu musical with script books in hand.

As a rule, Dean paid—and in cash, from a perpetual wad often exceeding $2,000. One notable exception was the night of Dean's birthday. Greg treated Dean to a Broadway showing of *Rent*. They talked on the phone every night for hours, yearning for more time together.

Soon, nightly phone calls weren't enough. The couple wanted to be together every night. They had the set-up that Greg had dreamed about—Greg's convenient midtown apartment near Penn Station and Dean's home outside of the city in the peace of Forest Hill.

By New York standards, their living expenses were quite low for a dual-dwelling pair. Greg's rent was reasonable. Dean rented out the top floor of his carriage house. After that money went toward his mortgage payment,

Dean only needed to shell out an additional $800 each month. The two spent weekends at Dean's house and stayed at Greg's place in Manhattan during the week.

Dean's weekday routine rarely varied. He slept away most of the morning and opened his office between noon and 1 P.M., Tuesday through Saturday. He worked until 8 or 9 o'clock at night. It was a smart business move to offer these unconventional hours. It allowed his clients to manage the expensive laser hair removal treatments with a bit more ease, since they did not have to take off work to get an appointment.

After Dean left the office for the evening, he usually stopped by the Equinox gym and lifted weights. Then, he'd grab dinner and take it back to Greg's apartment. Typically, he'd surf the Internet until sometime after midnight, then head off to bed. Quite the party boy in the eighties, Dean slowed down considerably in the late nineties as he approached his fortieth birthday. For a while, life for Greg and Dean was quiet and domestic.

Both men were open with their families about their relationship. They spent time together with them regularly, receiving affection and acceptance on both sides. "My mother loved Dean," Greg said, "because I loved him."

One day in October 1998, Greg Bach was stunned when, without any warning, Dean seemed to disappear off the face of the earth.

CHAPTER THIRTEEN

FRUSTRATED BY HER INABILITY TO FIND ANYONE WILLING TO stop Dean Faiello's illegal practice, Dr. Polis struggled to put the former employee out of her mind. Then she received a notice from a health insurance plan that listed her as a participating provider. "Why," they wanted to know, "are you writing so many prescriptions for Dean Faiello for Stadol?"

She paused for a moment to process the question. She was not familiar with that drug. She feared that a pad was stolen from her office and her signature forged. Dr. Polis called the company, telling them, "I have written no such prescription. I would like to see a copy of the actual script."

The health insurance office faxed her a copy and she knew right away that it was fraudulent. It was written on a page from an old pad she'd put in a bin for shredding some time ago—one with a defunct telephone number printed on it. She thought all of those old pads had been destroyed. The signature looked nothing like hers. Someone had to listen to her now; Dean's forgery violated the law without question.

This time, the Drug Enforcement Agency returned her call immediately. Now, they were interested. At their instruction, she visited three separate police precincts and filled out paperwork, reporting Dean's theft and forgery.

At one precinct, she overheard the officers mention Dr. Andrew Reyner as another physician connected to Dean. She assumed that he was a victim of theft, too. She had no idea that Dr. Reyner was a willing accomplice.

LAW ENFORCEMENT ATTENTION ZEROED IN ON DEAN FAIELLO. One of Dean's former employees confirmed that Dean had in fact stolen prescription pads from Dr. Polis before he left his job at her SoHo clinic. He also voiced suspicions that Dean was performing the types of laser surgery that require a medical license. Authorities arrested Dean and charged him with possession of a controlled substance, forgery and possession of a forged instrument.

Greg spent three days wondering and worrying about what happened to Dean before he got a call. Dean explained that he was at his sister Debra's house and that he'd been busted. His Dad, Sam, posted his bail and got him out of jail.

IN NOVEMBER, DEAN PLED GUILTY TO THE LESSER MISDE-meanor charge of possession of a forged instrument. The judge sentenced him to 3 years of probation and mandatory drug rehabilitation.

Dean spent six weeks in upstate New York receiving treatment at a clinic. When he returned home, Greg was waiting. He could not abandon Dean in his time of need—Greg loved him. Dean said to Greg, "If anything happens to me, I want to bequeath my house to you. You love this house more than I do." Greg was touched; it reinforced his belief in Dean's love.

Greg celebrated Dean's new sobriety by throwing a magnificent Christmas Eve dinner party for both of their families at the Newark house. As a professional event planner, Greg knew how to create the perfect occasion. The house and grounds were a Christmas wonderland once again. A tall, symmetrical Christmas tree covered with unique gold and red ornaments and tiny white lights set the mood. The dining room with its red walls was the centerpiece. The dining table sat before a large window and gleamed from the brilliant glow of wall sconces. On its surface, clusters of red roses and bows complemented silver serving pieces, crystal goblets rimmed with gold and bright white dinner plates on golden chasers. Madame Jeritza would have been delighted by Greg's holiday transformation of the home.

Dean's mother Carmel, his sister Debra and her partner, a New Jersey state public defender, mingled with Greg's parents and family. No one knew that Carmel Faiello's body—in remission from uterine cancer for years—was about to betray her once again.

SKINOVATIONS, ALTHOUGH DORMANT FOR WEEKS, WAS WAITING for Dean's return to pump up business and get income flowing. The time spent away from his office created serious financial difficulties. Greg loaned him $8,000 to get current on his mortgage payment.

Dean's new commitment to abstinence from drugs and alcohol made it possible for him to work hard and regain his footing. He expanded his work week to six days—Tuesday through Sunday—which, combined with longer work days, brought in the cash he needed to get up to date on his laser equipment leases and put his economic life back on track. He faithfully paid Greg $600 every month toward his debt.

Dean's CPE license lapsed at the end of 1998. He had not reported any CEUs (Continuing Education Units) to the American Electrology Association. Dean had taken classes but had not kept up on the paperwork. This lapse was not unusual for someone in his field. Many electrologists neglect to renew their membership in the organization and yet continue to practice, placing "CPE" after their names. The certification, after all, bears no legal significance. Many believe that once earned, a CPE is theirs in perpetuity.

A far more serious concern loomed in Dean's professional life, one he had no knowledge of at the time. His arrest for forging prescriptions attracted the notice of the Office of Professional Discipline—an agency within New York's Department of Education. On December 23, 1998, Kathy Hearn, an undercover operative of the agency, made an appointment with Dean.

She showed Dean a spot of discolored pigmentation. Dean diagnosed it as a benign skin lesion. Overstepping the medical bounds with this pronouncement posed a potential danger to the patient. Most doctors would advise a biopsy before coming to that conclusion and taking action. Instead, Dean offered to remove the lesion with laser treatments. She would not feel any pain during the procedure, he told her, because he would administer a local anesthetic. Again, Dean stepped into territory under the purview of licensed physicians, not cosmetic practitioners.

Hearn filed a report with her office. They referred the case to the office of the state Attorney General Eliot Spitzer for prosecution. Officials there decided not to press charges at that time because they wanted more evidence of wrong-doing. They encouraged the department of education to continue their investigation.

Dean dodged a bullet without even knowing how close it whizzed by his head. It looked like 1999 would be a great year—until fate intervened, driving Dean back to abuse of alcohol and then the harder stuff.

Early in the year, Carmel Faiello was diagnosed with a recurrence of cancer. Years before, doctors had diagnosed uterine cancer, but after surgery and radiation treatment, she went into remission. In 1999, she had a problem with her epiglottis—the flap of cartilage that lies behind the tongue and in front of the entrance to the larynx. At rest in its normal functioning, this valve-like structure remains upright, allowing air to pass through. During swallowing, it is supposed to fold back and cover the entrance to the windpipe.

Carmel's epiglottis was stuck in the upright position, allowing food and drink to enter the lungs, and air to enter her stomach. Doctors recommended surgery to repair the valve. When they made the incision, they discovered rampant cancer, including a large tumor in her stomach. Her condition was inoperable. They stitched her back together and left her to die.

Whenever Dean paid his mother a visit at Debra's house, he butted heads with his sister and her partner, who did not want Carmel to take sleeping pills. They wanted to provide holistic care for her in her final days.

Dean, however, agonized over his mother's pain and inability to sleep. He decided to slip her drugs without letting her, his sister or the doctor know. When Greg found out about it, it instigated their first fight.

It was on Greg's birthday. He spent the day expecting Dean to call. Every hour that the phone did not ring was a disappointment. It made Greg a little upset to spend his birthday all alone, but he wasn't angry with Dean. He knew his boyfriend's mother was dying, and his forgetfulness—although it saddened him—was understandable.

Late that night—with barely an hour of his special day left—the phone finally rang. Instead of wishing Greg a happy birthday, though, Dean launched into a diatribe about the difficulty of crushing up sleeping pills into his mother's gelato.

"Why are you doing that?" Greg asked.

"I can't let Mom or Debra know I'm giving them to her."

"You can't do that, Dean," Greg screamed. "You don't know what other medications she's taking. You don't know if the pills you're giving her will have a bad interaction with the other drugs."

"She can't sleep, Greg. She's in too much pain. I can't just sit here and watch her suffer."

"You can't drug people without their knowledge, Dean."

Dean slammed down the phone. Greg sighed. He knew Dean was acting out of compassion, but he also knew his actions could have deadly consequences.

DEAN HAD NOT YET CAUGHT UP WITH HIS BACKLOG OF BILLS. He had to work long hours. That kept him from visiting his mother as often as he would like. His absence at her bedside fed his guilt and increased his sense of frustration—a potentially destructive combination for any addict attempting to maintain sobriety.

Greg noticed Dean's descent in its early stages, but he hesitated to intervene, fearing that it would drive Dean deeper into dependency. Only in retrospect did Greg realize he'd become an enabler. At the time, though, he thought he was helping someone he loved. He knew Dean had genuine feelings for him, as well. Dean wanted to be sober for Greg. His success, though, was spotty, creating a dysfunctional trap for both men.

Greg tried to distract and re-focus Dean's attention by initiating a renovation project at the Newark home. The resulting look was elegant. Artfully placed mirrors enlarged the rooms. Scattered settees created nooks for conversation. A baby grand piano added panache.

Outside, he planted colorful beds of impatiens and other annuals. In addition to event planning, Greg's business included garden landscaping and maintenance contracts; whenever he over-bought boxwood hedges or any other shrubbery or flower, he worked them into the exterior design on Elwood.

From the beginning of their relationship, Greg developed a passion for revitalizing the grounds of the historic Victorian mansion. He loved having an outlet for his creative impulses—a place where he could experiment with plants and design as he pleased, without having to worry about the desires of a paying client. He placed an eclectic assortment of statuary on the grounds. He made the interior and the gardens a showcase. But no matter how hard he tried, he could not get Dean engaged in any constructive way.

As his mother's health worsened, Dean missed more and more days of work, sabotaging his own efforts at economic recovery. When Greg left for his annual vacation to his family's place on the lake in upstate New York, Dean lost control of any semblance of sobriety.

Carmel Faiello died on August 12, 1999—just two weeks before Dean's fortieth birthday. At great personal expense, Greg created the most lavish floral display he could conceive of for her funeral. He doubted the suburban funeral home had ever seen a piece that large. Greg stood by Dean's side offering comfort throughout the services at Grace Church. The death of a close relative devastated most HIV-positive individuals, reducing their sense of a safety net—creating a world where there was one less person who cared about their fate. Dean was no exception. After his mother's death, he withdrew into a drug-induced haze, sleeping whole days away.

Elizabeth, Dean's Hungarian housekeeper, grew increasingly concerned about Dean, too. He had stirred up her maternal instincts, making her as protective of him as she would be for a son. Even though she only worked weekdays, Elizabeth frequently dropped in on Sunday afternoons to make sure Dean was okay. She feared that she'd come to work one day and find him dead from a drug overdose.

Sam Faiello, Dean's father, was still estranged from his son. Dean never forgave him for his abusive behavior, or for divorcing his mother, or for the wounds inflicted when Dean came out of the closet.

Dean had made some effort to interact with his father while his mother was still alive. At her prodding, he called Sam on his birthday and on Father's Day. Now that his mother was gone, those efforts died, too.

As far as Dean was concerned, their relationship was scarred for life. No contact was necessary or even desirable. Nonetheless, Sam did show some paternal concern for his only son. He called Elizabeth often to find out how Dean was doing.

Greg could no longer remain silent in the face of Dean's deterioration. With the help of a mutual friend who was a physician, Greg got Dean back into rehab on an outpatient basis. Dean visited a Manhattan clinic three mornings a week.

Once again, Dean expressed a sincere desire to give up alcohol and drugs. His life eventually returned to an even keel—he worked hard, enjoyed life and made progress in resurrecting his economic stability.

Greg expected that Dean would receive some inheritance from his mother, which would ease some of his financial difficulties. Debra, though, inherited everything. Greg asked him why he didn't get a share of his mother's estate. Dean shrugged and said, "Because I'm so irresponsible with money." What Greg didn't know was that, in a sense, Dean received his inheritance in advance. Before his mother passed away, Dean applied for and got a number of credit cards in his mother's name. He maxed out every one of them.

After Carmel's death, the bills came in, revealing Dean's

fraud. The estate paid thousands of dollars to clear the debt Dean had incurred. No one pressed charges.

Greg believed that if he could ferret out the root cause of Dean's addiction, if he could uncover a traumatic incident in his childhood, then he could guide him through the self-examination and confession that are often the first step to healing. In this way, he felt Dean could make meaningful and abiding changes in his life. "Why do you need to abuse drugs and alcohol?" Greg asked him.

Dean's only response was a shrug.

"Why are you so unhappy?"

Dean brushed off the question with a non-answer: "I was born unhappy."

Then, a lawsuit disrupted Dean's peace of mind and his fragile hold on sobriety. Former patient Mark Schuckman sued Dean for $8,000, claiming that the laser treatments Dean used to remove hair from his back were useless— Dean's promises of results were bogus. Since laser was not as effective with hair removal on the upper torso as it was on the lower half of the body, it was unclear whether Dean or the technology were at fault. Nonetheless, after months of wrangling, the suit was settled. In addition to attorney fees, Dean had to pay Schuckman $3,250. It was a blow to Dean's bottom line and to his battle against addiction.

Again, Dean embraced his old habits of drugs, alcohol and escapism. Again, substance abuse only served to feed the demons and make them stronger.

CHAPTER FOURTEEN

JASON OPSAHL RETURNED TO NEW YORK IN 1998, HIS REGImen of chemotherapy complete. He stopped by the offices of Broadway Cares/Equity Fights AIDS to offer his services as a volunteer. There he met Peter Borzotta. Peter had heard of Jason and knew of his battle with cancer. He thought Jason seemed thin, even gaunt, and the ravages of chemo were etched into his face. But both his spirits and his energy level were high.

The two men hit if off right away and soon were seeing each other outside of the BC/EFA offices. As their relationship grew, they opened up about their pasts. Jason told Peter about his previous boyfriend Dean Faiello and how Dean's problems with drugs destroyed their relationship.

Jason seemed as healthy as ever, singing and dancing his way back to the stage in the off-Broadway production of *Captains Courageous*. He performed through the full run of the show in the Manhattan Theatre Club, from its opening on February 16, 1999, to its final curtain less than two months later on April 4.

That year, Jason was one of the five dancers in a production team assisting the creative process as Jerry Mitchell choreographed routines for *The Full Monty*. During this project, the dancers often relaxed in the basement. Jason entertained, doing crazy dance routines borrowed from his days at the Disney theme parks. He took those moves over the top, his lean 6′2″ body forming joyous contortions as he clowned his way through the impromptu routine. Jerry often joined in. The two men danced until they were laughing so hard they could no longer stand.

The Full Monty moved to San Diego for a three-month run. Jason, for minor reasons, was not one of the players on the West Coast. But when the show made its triumphant return, he rejoined the cast, earning him his greatest fame. He was a "swing" in this production—always ready to perform any of the five different parts during the eight performances each week.

On opening night, the honor of the Gypsy Robe fell on his shoulders—a tradition dating back to the 1950 production of *Gentlemen Prefer Blondes*. Jason earned his place in this ceremonial celebration as the chorus member with the most Broadway musical show credits.

Half an hour before curtain, the robe was delivered to his dressing room. He slipped it on and circled the stage three times while cast members surrounded him, reaching out to touch the robe for good luck. Jason then made the traditional tour of each dressing room. Since *Full Monty* was the first musical to open on Broadway that season, the garment was a plain, full-length dressing gown. After the performance, Jason added a memento from the show to the robe, wrote the opening date and passed it around for cast members to sign. The robe remained in Jason's custody until opening night of the next musical on Broadway—a revival of *The Rocky Horror Show* on November 15. At that time, he visited the NSU Theater and bestowed the robe on the new Gypsy.

The world looked bright for Jason. On September 24, 2001, he took part in *Dreamgirls*, the one-night twentieth anniversary benefit concert for the Actors' Fund at the Ford Center for Performing Arts.

In December 2001, Jason faced a recurrence of his brain cancer. He underwent more surgery. Surviving the risky procedure in the operating room was only the first challenge. Afterwards, he endured round after round of exhausting, nauseating chemotherapy. But Jason never complained. He never whined. He never indulged in self-pity.

Rosie O'Donnell came to his rescue one more time. While Jason battled his illness, Rosie gave him money for food and rent and helped with his medical bills.

Jason returned to New York in time for the tenth annual *Broadway Bares* show, but he was bald and uncomfortable with the appearance of his chemo-ravaged body. The opening song that year, "The Barest Show on Earth," was a reprise of the opener from the seventh show. Jason performed that song three years earlier—his voice perfect for the number. Jerry Mitchell could not imagine featuring the song again unless Jason performed it. As self-conscious as Jason was about his appearance, he could not say no. He stood before the audience and gave a stellar rendition. Those who knew him were stunned by his incredible strength and determination to carry on in the face of his monumental struggle.

In the spring of 2002, Jason participated in the 16th Annual Easter Bonnet Competition. A six-week fundraiser for Broadway Cares/Equity Fights AIDS, designers for Broadway, off-Broadway and touring companies created elaborate bonnets, and the casts created and performed an entertaining presentation.

Rosie O'Donnell opened the show with 98-year-old showgirl Doris Eaton Travis. When she returned at the end of the show, Jason handed her a large bouquet of flowers and said, "You have been our cheerleader. You've been our spokeswoman. Thank you, Rosie."

Jason returned to the cast of *The Full Monty*, performing in the rigorous eight-times-a-week schedule. He took oral chemotherapy drugs at the same time, keeping the show going until the final curtain on September 1, 2002.

CHAPTER FIFTEEN

DEAN'S LIFE PATH AFTER JASON WAS NOT AS TRAGIC, BUT IT was definitely more dismal. He went to work fewer days than he stayed home, stewing in a blue funk. The more he blew off work, the worse he shattered any hope of attaining financial equilibrium. In 2001, the mortgage payments on his home in Newark were seriously in arrears again. Foreclosure loomed. Dean needed a large infusion of cash to get back on track.

Meanwhile, Greg wanted some assurance of reimbursement before shelling out more of his money. He proposed that they rent out the third floor of the house, the tenants paying Greg directly to reduce the amount Dean owed him. Dean agreed. The upstairs was rented out to a young married couple, and Greg loaned Dean another $7,000.

The new loan could have been a sore point for Dean and Greg. After all, Greg did want to be paid back eventually and Dean still frittered away his own money on drugs. Nonetheless, Dean continued to pay $600 each month toward his debt to Greg and the couple got along well.

To help scrape money together, Dean rented one of the four bedrooms on the second floor to a medical student who was more often at school, the hospital or the library than he was at home. Dean and Greg barely noticed his presence.

In fact, Dean depended on Greg. He spent work nights in Greg's apartment and relied on Greg to wake him up and get him off to work. If Greg was not there in the morning to do that, Dean slept through appointments and drove his receptionist to distraction, rescheduling and making excuses.

When Greg planned his annual escape to the family home on the lake that summer, the receptionist pleaded with him not to go. Greg had close ties to his family and this annual reunion mattered to him a great deal. So in an attempt to keep Dean as sober as possible during Greg's absence, Debra stepped in to watch over him. Dean spent his weekends at her home in Milford, New Jersey, and she called Greg's apartment on workday mornings to get Dean out of bed. Greg and Debra jokingly referred to this arrangement as Dean's baby-sitting service.

Dean was still in casual contact with Jason Opsahl in the fall of 2001. Jason told Dean that he was moving from his studio apartment in the high-rise building at 449 West 44th Street to more luxurious digs in a new complex on River Place. Dean knew that residential buildings in New York were required to provide some low-rent housing units. He busied himself with the paperwork needed to qualify and acquire Jason's old apartment at a discounted rate. He won eligibility, moving in for only $1,550 per month. It was a remarkably low amount for its location and the quality of the unit, but still it was an expense that Dean could ill afford. Sure, it was nicer and roomier than Greg's crowded place—but he could stay with Greg for free.

Moving into the West 44th Street apartment created an additional problem: Dean overslept nearly every day. He had the sense to know that there was one appointment he dared not miss—the one with his probation officer. Dean always spent the night before one of these required monthly appearances at Greg's apartment.

On a typical work day though, he spent the night at his apartment and arrived late to work. This prompted his receptionist to call Greg and plead with him to wake up Dean and get him into the office. Those demands disrupted Greg's work day; but still, he walked the fourteen blocks to Dean's new home to rouse him from bed. He did, after all, have his own financial interests to protect. As long as Dean went to work each day, Greg had a hope of repayment. And as long as they maintained regular contact, there was a possibility of preserving a hold—albeit a tenuous one—on their floundering relationship.

That hope for the relationship and the repayment, though, diminished with each passing day. Dean stopped paying on his loan and Greg was outraged. In disgust, he stopped responding when asked to provide wake-up service.

Dean struggled to meet his own basic needs. There was simply not enough income rolling in for him to survive the added expense of a Manhattan apartment, no matter how good a bargain he had. His solution was to attempt to rent the house in Newark. He found an interested couple, thinking his income shortfall was solved. But driving to Forest Hills in their rented moving van, they got lost and meandered through some of the grittier Newark neighborhoods. After that eye-opening experience, the couple reneged on their agreement.

Eventually, Dean stopped showing up for work entirely. His alarmed receptionist notified Greg. After calling Dean's apartment numerous times without response, Greg went to 44th Street and buzzed up to Dean. Still no response, day after day.

After nearly a week, Greg was frantic. He contacted a doctor he knew socially and convinced him to intervene.

The doctor left a message on Dean's answering machine: "Dean, if you do not let us into the apartment, I'll call the police. They'll force their way in."

The next time Greg went to the apartment, Dean responded to the buzzer. Greg went in to find the apartment looking like a disaster zone. Dean had been inside all along, buzzed out on a drug binge.

MEANWHILE, DR. LAURIE POLIS' STAR WAS RISING HIGH IN THE Manhattan horizon. Her business, now named the SoHo Skin and Laser Dermatology Group, flourished. The location of her office complex was ideal—SoHo had become home to the most prestigious spas in the world, and Dr. Polis stepped into that arena with the opening of her Mezzanine Spa in 2000.

She reigned over this world, with the sort of cachet that drew a long list of celebrity clients. Dr. Polis was named one of the seven most sought-after dermatologists in New York City.

The glamorous spa she created was an oasis of delight. Walls with Japanese grass–infused wallpaper, other walls of rice paper, bamboo floors, a three-story water sculpture and a lounge stocked with wasabi snacks and fortune cookies formed an exquisite backdrop for her services. A dozen doctors now worked at her facility. In addition to a medical practice in cosmetic, clinical and surgical dermatology, she offered a Western menu featuring cutting-edge skin-care treatments based on the latest science and tailored to the needs of each individual, as well as an Eastern menu offering Ayuveda from India, a philosophy-based holistic approach to health and healing that utilized herbs and meditation; acupressure; and Chinese herbal facials and relaxation therapies. Dr. Polis oversaw the most comprehensive medical day spa in the country.

One day, she flipped through a new issue of *New York*

magazine. Her fingers froze in disbelief and dismay. Once again she stared at an ad for SkinOvations. Dean was still at it, in a new office, but still offering the same services, presented with the same marketing approach.

She felt helpless and frustrated. *Why wasn't he in jail?*

DEAN'S THREE YEARS PROBATION FOR FORGING PRESCRIPTIONS expired in January 2002. He was now free and clear of the criminal courts and the justice system. Or so he thought.

Authorities, however, had other ideas. On February 2, Daniel Kelleher, director of investigations for the state department of education, sent a second undercover officer, Ariana Miller, to visit Dean in his offices. He hoped that this time they would get sufficient evidence to convince the attorney general's office to move forward with the prosecution of Dean Faiello.

Dean offered to remove blood vessels from Ariana's leg and diagnosed her skin lesion as benign. He told her he could remove both with a laser, and that she would not feel any pain because he would inject her with a local anesthetic before starting the procedure. When she questioned his credentials, he assured her that he was a doctor.

Tonya Holder, yet another investigator, entered Dean's office on March 22. He also diagnosed her skin lesions as benign, again offering to remove them with a laser after injecting the area with anesthetic. He gave her the same assurances that he was in fact medically qualified to perform the procedure.

The investigators prepared a second round of reports and filed them with the office of Attorney General Eliot Spitzer in May, then sat back and waited for him to take action and put Dean out of business.

That summer, Dean moved the offices of SkinOvations to a new space at 117 East 18th Street. This Gramercy Park–area property was owned by his personal physician,

Dr. Lawrence Fontana. Dean worked there under the supervision of a doctor in the neighboring suite, Dr. Frank Spinelli. Spinelli provided comprehensive adult primary care with a focus on gay health. As a specialist in treating HIV-positive patients, he was in great demand in the gay community. His clientele also appreciated him for his good looks. The *New York Blade* named him one of the two hottest doctors in town. "Those dark, brooding eyes. That curly hair. That muscled body. Oh yeah, he's also a great doctor," the Manhattan gay newspaper wrote.

Despite the fresh start in an office complex with a respected doctor, Dean's behavior continued to deteriorate. He never seemed to sleep. He spent his nights reading medical websites instead. His mood swings were more sudden than an earthquake and more extreme than a category-five hurricane.

Greg knew that drug use, complicated by lack of sleep, provided the fuel for Dean's erratic and bizarre behavior. Dean, though, tried to conceal his habit. Greg bumped into confirmation wherever he turned—a Pyrex plate with a straw in it stuffed in a linen closet, a Stadol inhaler shoved deep down in the trash.

Greg still tried to engage him in conversation about the root of his problems, but once again made little or no progress. He consulted with experts at rehab centers. Greg wanted desperately to save Dean from himself. He also had the growing suspicion that Dean was courting trouble by passing himself off as a physician. He saw more and more mail coming in addressed to Dr. Dean Faiello, M.D.

One evening, that worry received confirmation. Greg dropped by Dean's office and together they walked out to the parking garage. A worker there said, "Goodnight, Dr. Faiello."

On the way home, Greg asked, "Dean, you don't tell people you're a doctor, do you?"

"No, of course not," Dean said.

"You know how much trouble you can get into if you do, don't you?"

Dean waved him off, dismissing his concern. Dean did not feel it was important. But he should have. While he made little of Greg's worries, a dark cloud churned over Dean's head. Lightning poised, ready to strike. The attorney general's office was receiving and responding to reports from the state department of education. Investigators from that office now dogged Dean's every step.

CHAPTER SIXTEEN

DEAN AND HIS BUSINESS ATTRACTED MORE THAN JUST AN official investigation. Two tenacious journalists now shadowed him, preparing to con the con.

Barbara Nevins Taylor, an investigative reporter with Channel 9 News, was the first to pick up the scent of the developing story. A native New Yorker, Barbara was born and raised in Queens. She attended New York City's Performing Arts High School—later named LaGuardia High School. She majored in sociology at Queens College, the City University of New York. By the time she graduated, Barbara planned to enter the world of journalism, following in the footsteps of her father, Zeke Segal, national assignment editor and southern bureau chief with CBS News.

Like many aspiring reporters, Barbara embarked on a journey of voluntary exile, polishing her craft in smaller media markets. She started as a reporter for WHNT, a television station in Huntsville, Alabama. She then worked as an anchor and reporter at WKYT in Lexington, Kentucky. She stepped into a substantially larger market when she snagged a reporter's position at a local television station in Atlanta, Georgia.

During this stop in her nomadic existence, Barbara met Nick Taylor, a long-time print journalist working in television news as a political reporter. Nick left broadcasting to take a position with the Jimmy Carter campaign and the two saw little of each other. But after Carter's successful election, Nick and Barbara started dating. Barbara was now the chief political correspondent at WAGA in Atlanta.

Nick and Barbara lived together for five and a half years and were then married in 1984. At last, Barbara was able to return home to New York—her journeyman dues paid—when she accepted a reporting job at WCBS.

Nick thrived in New York. He was elected president of the Authors Guild and successfully authored twelve non-fiction books including one, *Laser: The Inventor, the Nobel Laureate, and the Thirty-Year Patent War*, about the technology that played such a pivotal role in Dean Faiello's professional life. Together, Nick and Barbara traveled, sailed and tackled the greatest challenges of the boomer generation: caring for the lives, bodies and minds of their elderly parents, and watching as they shrunk before their eyes.

In 1992, Barbara left WCBS, taking a hiatus from the frenetic pace of television journalism and devoting her attention to her foster child. When she returned to media work in 1994, she found her mission as an investigative reporter at the New York–based, Fox-owned television station, Channel 9.

She tackled an FBI sting operation gone bad, stolen identity stories, and gun-related crime. She exposed a green card scam that bilked immigrants out of nearly a million dollars. She uncovered an unscrupulous landlord—one who didn't provide heat or hot water and refused to repair collapsed ceilings, giant holes in the floors, leaky roofs and broken toilets. She was there with a cameraman, bringing viewers the image of this man as he was handcuffed and carted off to jail. She unraveled the flim-flam operations of unscrupulous tax preparers, fly-by-night contractors, towing companies who stole cars and phony mortgage companies who stole houses.

Through all this work, the praise piled high for Barbara Nevins Taylor. She earned thirteen Emmys, a "Laurel" from the *Columbia Journalism Review* and other honors from the Associated Press, the Society of Professional Journalists, the Deadline Club, The Newswomen's Club of New York, the New Jersey Broadcasters Association and the New York Society of the Silurians.

When Barbara focused her talents and energies on the cosmetic surgery industry, she stepped onto a path that would lead her to Dean Faiello.

Initially, her story focused on three physicians—one in New Jersey and two in Queens—who were the subject of repeated complaints from viewers whose plastic surgeries were botched. The most egregious offender was Dr. Jose Arely Lopez. She looked into his practice at a time when he was about to lose his license for the death of one of his patients. Wanda Nunez, a young mother, died on the operating table because of the anesthesia Dr. Lopez administered during a tummy tuck procedure.

Women who survived his surgeries told tales of horrible pain and disfigurement. Carol Brown went to Dr. Lopez's New Jersey office for liposuction on her stomach and legs. After the procedure, she had open lacerations on her torso. Lopez told her nothing was wrong—her wounds would heal and disappear.

Several months later, when she expressed her dissatisfaction again, Lopez recommended corrective laser surgery to remove the excessive scarring. Carol underwent the procedure with Diana, Dr. Lopez's wife, assisting him in surgery. Diana had no medical training at all.

Afterwards, the burning pain Carol felt was intense, and the disfigurement was not alleviated—if anything, it worsened. When she sought a second opinion, Carol was told that further treatment was useless, and she was scarred for life.

Maria Linarez visited Dr. Lopez for liposuction, too. He performed the procedure on her back—once again with the assistance of his unschooled wife. The surgery left a legacy of scars and pain, both physical and mental. Maria believed she looked like a monster.

When authorities revoked his medical credentials, Lopez closed his existing office and calmly set up another on Fifth Avenue in Manhattan. Barbara made repeated efforts to send in an undercover operative to catch Lopez in the act, but always failed to get an appointment. Then, she caught on to the process. All prospective patients were screened by Lopez's brother—if you were not a Latino, you didn't get in to see him.

Barbara lined up the right bait and the trap was set. The television station offered the attorney general's office the opportunity to provide an undercover investigator to accompany them on the appointment, but they declined.

Channel 9's hidden camera caught the professionally defrocked Dr. Lopez doling out medical advice and offering to perform procedures to make the phony patient "more beautiful." Now they had proof that Lopez was violating the law, but it seemed like the authorities were never going to make a move. On the day the story was scheduled to air, Barbara and her cameraman barged into Dr. Lopez's offices. They caught him on tape in the middle of surgery with his hands in a patient's body.

They called the police. Dr. Lopez raced out a side door and into the street. The crew followed him outside where, to Barbara's amazement, Lopez denied being the person performing the surgery they just witnessed and recorded.

Channel 9 aired the story that night as Dr. Lopez fled to Florida. There, he set up a new practice and got busy risking the lives of more people. The attorney general's office moved swiftly when they learned of his location, and extradited him back to New York. Lopez pled guilty to practicing medicine without a license and received a sentence of 2 to 6 years in the New York state prison system.

While covering the Lopez story, Barbara expanded her focus to encompass the cosmetic surgery industry as a whole, including the proliferation of laser use by people outside of the medical profession. The pieces produced and aired as a result of these investigations prompted a patient of Dean Faiello to call the station's hot line, claiming that Dean told his clients that he was a physician. Here was an individual who was not just using laser in possibly illegal ways, but who was also pretending to be a doctor. Barbara believed this situation posed a huge threat to the public. She placed a call to Dr. Laurie Polis, who filled her in on Dean Faiello's history.

In August 2002, Linda Sachs, a Channel 9 producer, made an appointment with the imposter. Using a hidden camera, she and the videographer caught Dean passing himself off as a physician. Barbara knew she had a hot story now. It was time to dig deeper.

CHAPTER SEVENTEEN

ANOTHER DOGGED MEMBER OF THE MEDIA ENTERED THE fray—Jeane MacIntosh of the *New York Post*. She moved in to research and write the story after getting a tip from a *New York Times* reporter who had interviewed Dr. Polis. The writer submitted a story about bogus skin care doctors that the *Times* turned down for publication because it was too sensational. She provided several names to Jeane, who chose to pursue information about one of the doctors in particular—Dean Faiello—when she learned he was under investigation by the Office of Professional Discipline.

Jeane was an Army brat born on May 21, 1961, in Munich, Germany. She grew up in Michigan and graduated from Miami University in Oxford, Ohio, with a degree in English in 1983. Like many English majors before her, she faced a limited number of options for employment and so she worked as a bartender for a while, much to her parents' dismay. One of her customers at the bar was the manager of a Detroit-area chain of suburban newspapers. She asked him for a job, to get her parents off of her back. He hired her and Jeane started her career in journalism writing for the *Northville Record* and the *Brighton Argus*.

A few months later, she accepted a job with a "crappy little newspaper" in New Jersey, where she lasted for two weeks, then quit and moved to Boston. There, she wrote copy for a mutual fund group. In 1985, she returned to the newspaper business as a financial writer and business reporter for *Women's Wear Daily*. She stuck with that employer for ten years.

Her next position was deputy editor of the *New York Post*'s Page Six, in 1995. As a contributor to the notorious and salacious gossip column, Jeane developed her contacts and learned to dish with the best. It was a glamorous job—nights of star-studded parties, days of celebrities whispering deep secrets in her ears.

The *Post* was part of Rupert Murdoch's media empire. Jeane took advantage of one perk of working for that massive conglomerate—an exchange program that enables reporters to work for other publications in the group for a short time.

Jeane chose a newspaper in Australia, where she worked for four months. There, she hit it off with an Australian reporter. While they were involved, she thought the romance was the real thing. However, when she returned to the United States, the relationship died faster than it began. To the Australian, Jeane was only another conquest— a momentary fling with a woman from the States. The situation was far more serious for Jeane—both romantically and in the long term. Upon her return, she discovered that she was pregnant with his child. Jeane considered her options and told herself, "Hey, I'm 37 years old. How hard can this be?" She decided to raise the child as a single mother.

In March 1998, other gossip columnists reported that Jeane was six months pregnant with the child of another Rupert Murdoch employee. In response to questions, Jeane said, "I'm spawning a hybrid tabloid warrior."

When Jean's little girl was 6 months old, Tom Parker stepped back into her life. She'd known Tom in high school. She'd even attended his first wedding, telling herself that if he was ever available again, she would marry him. He was available now and the romance began.

Her personal life entered a gratifying phase, but professionally the going got rough. The destructive impact of her seemingly frivolous job hit hard in November 1999. Jeane reported on the life of talent agent Jay Moloney.

She wrote a piece about his cocaine addiction and how it drove him from a position running Paradise Music into a rehabilitation clinic. Within hours of the story's release, the reverberations struck an already depressed Jay. He wrapped a belt around the shower nozzle and then around his neck, killing himself. Jay's friend Dana Grachetto was more than happy to talk to the media, describing how he warned Jeane that if she published the story, it would push Jay over the edge.

The controversy wounded Jeane, and in December 1999, she and her toddler daughter left New York to join Tom Parker in the more peaceful Midwestern environment of Chicago. The *Post* did not want to lose Jeane and offered her a part-time job as Midwest correspondent. Her original agreement called for three days of work each month. Soon, though, the demand for her services expanded to twenty days a month, the *Post* flying her to Texas, North Dakota, Minnesota and elsewhere to cover stories. Meanwhile, she wrote freelance stories for Chicago magazines, covering weightier stories than the typical celebrity fluff, like a high-profile prostitution scandal—one that also brought a suicide threat to her door. Fortunately, this time, another dead body was not laid at her feet.

She referred to herself as a "recovering gossip columnist" and vowed she would never return to that work again. "Some days," she wrote, "I don't regret leaving at all. Other days I miss Page Six: it's like a phantom limb that I keep groping for, and I'm still surprised when I realize it's not there."

Then *Women's Wear Daily* made her an offer she couldn't refuse—a job she could fit in with her responsibilities to the *Post*. They wanted her to write a bi-weekly column on fashion industry gossip for the launch of their new website. Jeane was hooked again on the gossip habit. "Obviously, the world cannot exist without gossip and neither can I." They produced one or two issues of the zine before 9-11. After that, the project fizzled into nothing.

Soon she and Tom were married and in early 2002, the *Post* urged Jeane back to New York to work as a general assignment and crime writer.

Jeane agreed and the family found a place in Hell's Kitchen, then eventually moved to a home in New Jersey.

In the flamboyant and provocative language of the *Post*, Jeane wrote stories about serial killers, cult leaders, bigamist barbers, child killers, battered but wealthy wives, and sects who abused children. She reported on pivotal events like the tsunami disaster of December 2004. Jeane finally she made her mark with her coverage of the Elizabeth Smart story, which would evolve into a book.

IN SEPTEMBER, BARBARA NEVINS TAYLOR LEARNED THAT THE state was also investigating Dean Faiello. Their probe was prompted by complaints from Dr. Laurie Polis, Dean's former employer, and Dr. Roy Geronemus, a physician who claimed he treated a number of patients whose procedures were botched by Dean.

Now three separate entities—Channel 9, the *Post*, and the state—staked out the 18th Street office. By September, each had figured out who the other players were, exchanging frequent waves and nods. It was a race to see who would get to the finish line first. The attorney general's office was at a disadvantage in this contest. They needed enough evidence to convict. The media outlets only needed enough to protect themselves should a lawsuit arise after the story had broken.

BARBARA MADE AN APPOINTMENT WITH DEAN FAIELLO. AGAIN, the Channel 9 news department extended an invitation to the attorney general's office to come along as an observer. Again, authorities declined.

Barbara entered Dean's offices with a hidden camera. The visit began with a consultation. Dean interviewed Barbara about what she wanted and documented her medical history. Then, he examined her features. "You could benefit from laser resurfacing on your face. To do that, though, I would want to have the other doctor here to participate, since it is a very complicated procedure," he said, referring to Dr. Frank Spinelli. He went on to explain that on his own, he could use the laser to remove beauty marks or moles. Barbara asked him about the spider veins in her legs. "They can easily be removed with laser," Dean said.

"Are you a doctor?"

"Um-hum, yeah," he said.

Barbara noticed that he appeared drowsy and slow, as if he were medicated. *Is this just his manner?* she wondered. *Or is he on drugs?*

Later in the visit, she repeated her query in her best imitation of an airhead: "So, you're a doctor, so I can trust you? I don't, I don't have to worry?"

Dean nodded his head. "Everything will be fine," he said.

"Where did you go to medical school?"

"I went to the University of Medicine and Dentistry of New Jersey," Dean said.

He then escorted Barbara into the treatment room where he showed her his laser equipment and demonstrated how he would apply it to her leg. He didn't explain the medical procedures as a doctor would; he just told her what he could do and how he would do it.

Barbara left his office ready to write her story, edit her tape and hit the air. Investigators from the attorney general's office, though, asked her to hold the story—an arrest was imminent.

MEANWHILE, JANE MACINTOSH, HEARING DEAN WAS GAY, traipsed down to Christopher Street and flashed his picture around. She learned about his former job at The Beach and also heard about his drug problem. She staked out a club he was said to frequent, but Dean remained elusive.

Surprisingly, Jeane had a skin lesion on her left arm. It looked as if it could be malignant. A physician performed a biopsy, and though the results were negative, without that testing, she would have run a huge risk having it removed: if it had been cancer, the excision would have destroyed the outward indications of malignancy, allowing it to spread unseen to other parts of the body.

Jeane took advantage of the situation and made an appointment with Dean for a consultation. He told her that he could remove it with two or three laser sessions. The charge for each treatment was $250. In response to her questions, he assured her that he was a doctor and detailed his credentials, just as he had done for Barbara.

Then Jeane asked the really important question: "Does it need to be biopsied?"

"No. There's no need for a biopsy," Dean said.

"Even though I have a history of cancer?"

"There is nothing to worry about," he assured her.

TO A HANDFUL OF PHONY PATIENTS FROM THE MEDIA, AND TO the authorities, Dean admitted to using the anesthetic lidocaine, the sedative Diprivan and the highly addictive synthetic narcotic fentanyl in the course of his treatments. There was no longer any doubt that his actions were criminal. But Barbara sat on her scoop until the arrest date, getting more impatient with each passing day. She knew Jeane MacIntosh was ready to publish her story in the *New York Post*. Barbara had to break the story first.

On the day of the planned arrest, Barbara couldn't wait any longer. She and a crew went down to Dean Faiello's office.

DEAN AND GREG STAYED AT GREG'S APARTMENT IN TOWN ON the night of Monday, September 30. The next morning before Dean left for work, the phone rang. It was his receptionist.

"There's a camera crew at the door wanting to come into the office," she warned.

"You can't let them in there," Dean told her.

The crew—and particularly Barbara Nevins Taylor—intimidated her. She told Dean that Barbara would not go away.

"Put her on the phone," Dean said.

Dean listened to what Barbara had to say, then, hoping she would just leave, he told her, "I don't want you in the office with cameras."

Dean hurried off to the office and when Barbara spotted him, she rushed toward him, putting a microphone to his face. "Why are you practicing medicine without a license?" she asked.

"Oh, I'm not," he said. "It's not so. It's simply not so." He pushed past Barbara and went into his office.

When he returned home that night, the stress was written in the furrows of his brow. He told Greg that he did not understand why he was singled out for an investigation—why anyone wanted to shut down his business, why he was under attack.

Channel 9 broke the story first on Friday, October 4. They aired portions of Barbara's hidden-camera video from her visit to Dean's office. The story contained a short clip of Dr. Laurie Polis saying, "Yes, this sounds like practicing medicine without a license."

Soon, Barbara's attention drifted away from the great pretender. She had exposed Dean Faiello to her viewers and to law enforcement. The authorities, she believed, would pick up where she left off, preventing Dean from posing as a doctor again. He presented no further threat to public safety.

JEANE MACINTOSH PAID ONE LAST VISIT TO DEAN, CATCHING him on the street corner by his office. "Dean, you told me that you were a doctor."

"I did not. I am not a doctor and never said I was. My website never referred to me as a doctor. You may have misunderstood me. If I was unclear or made that mistake, I apologize." As he spoke, he looked her in the eye with unwavering intensity and delivered his denials with all the appearance of pure sincerity. He was so convincing that Jeane, who'd been lied to by the best, began to doubt herself. She had to listen to the audiotape of her under-cover visit again to make sure she had not misconstrued the meaning of his words.

The *New York Post* broke the story in print that Sunday. The story quoted Dr. Polis: "Having a laser in your hand is like having a gun. You need to know what you're doing. You can get a mole lasered off by one of these practition-ers and three years later, you're dead of brain cancer." Jeane's headline for the story read: "He'll Make Your Skin Crawl."

CHAPTER EIGHTEEN

DEBRA FAIELLO READ ABOUT HER BROTHER'S LATEST MISADventures in the *Post*. She drove over to Dean's home to talk to him and make a plan.

Having a brother in this kind of trouble had to be difficult for Debra. She seemed such a straight arrow. She attended Rutgers University, where she played softball. After graduation, she became a New Jersey State Trooper. While in the state police force, she entered the K-9 unit as a dog handler. She and her German shepherd Xena were well trained in drug and bomb detection. They even participated in canine blood drives.

As a sergeant, Debra was the training coordinator for the K-9 units in the state's Explosives Detection and Render Safe Task Force. This statewide partnership between bomb squads and K-9 handlers developed as a program of the state's Domestic Security Preparedness Task Force in October 2001 in response to the September 11 attacks.

Debra probably would have preferred running that day—she made very decent time in 5K races—but instead she was in Newark trying to help her brother cope with a mess of his own making.

Greg, meanwhile, had shelled out a $7,500 retainer to hire lawyer Margaret Shalley for Dean. Shalley, a native New Yorker who earned her bachelor's degree at SUNY's

Binghamton University was a graduate of Washington College of Law at American University in Washington, D.C. After thirteen years in public sector work, Shalley established her private practice in 1997. Dean was one in a string of disreputable clients that included a *Newsday* circulation manager accused of fraud for inflating distribution numbers, and a former senior spokesman in New York for the ousted Taliban government, charged with tax evasion for failing to report all of his income. Unlike others she encountered in her work, Dean was polite, charming and intelligent. He expressed a genuine concern for other people and demonstrated a deep-seated desire to help them.

With his new attorney by his side, Dean turned himself in to the attorney general's office in Manhattan at 7:40 on the morning of Tuesday, October 8, 2002. In short order, she would validate the faith Greg placed in her.

RONDA LUSTMAN REPRESENTED THE STATE IN THE PROSECUTION of Dean Faiello. Over more than twenty years, her body of work in combating the unlicensed practice of medicine in New York helped define the legal boundaries of this crime. In addition, she worked on other medically-related matters, representing the state against pharmacies selling drugs without a doctor's prescription, the practice of dentistry without a license, the theft of dental licensing exams and charges of fraud and grand larceny against a nurse for operating an illegal health plan.

She was dedicated to protecting the public, and the prosecution of Dean Faiello fell into her area of specialization. Dean would face a seasoned professional in court—one who, if anything, was over-qualified to handle his E class felony.

On his way from Central Booking to the courthouse, Dean spotted the *New York Post* investigator who played a role in his fall. Giving her his winning, smile he said, "Good morning, Miss MacIntosh."

When she asked him about Dr. Polis' allegations, he said: "I have the greatest respect for Dr. Polis, but she was very upset because I left her practice. I was doing treatments. I was pretty successful. And I wanted to start my own business." He didn't mention that he told Dr. Polis that he was dying of AIDS.

Dean was arraigned on October 8, 2002, in New York Supreme Court in Manhattan on three charges of the unlicensed practice of medicine, based on consultations with the undercover operatives for the attorney general's office, Investigators Kathy Hearn, Ariana Miller and Tonya Holder. Eleven more unlicensed practices charges were brought against him for each time he treated Jill Vasquez and three more for every time Sandra Corinthian visited his office. Additionally, he faced three counts of assault in the second degree related to his treatment of Sandra. The assault charge at that lower level could signify minor pain or bruises. In this case, Dean's removal of Sandra's tattoo left scars that were more unsightly than the original inked art. These were all relatively minor felony charges, but still punishable by a prison term of one to four years each.

The judge set bail at $5,000. He also set one firm condition for Dean's release and continued freedom while awaiting trial. Dean could not continue to treat *any* patients—not with the legal use of laser for hair removal, not even with other laser use under the supervision of a licensed medical practitioner. The judge forbade him from working with lasers under any conditions.

Before release, Dean had to raise the money for bail. Sam Faiello, who reappeared from out of their estrangement to observe Dean's arraignment, asked Margaret Shalley, "Why don't we just leave him there and see if a

night in jail will straighten him up?" Greg was aghast
at Sam's solution. Looking back, he realized how little
he knew about Dean's history of irresponsibility. Greg
stepped up again for Dean. The bondsman required cash,
and Greg got a cash advance of $2,500 from his credit
card and delivered it to the bail company's office. The
bond firm covered the other half of the bail money. Dean
returned home late in the afternoon of that same day.

The next day, Dean left Newark and headed over to his
office near Gramercy Park. Greg thought he planned to
pack up his belongings and close down his office. Dean,
however, had other ideas. He had a client to treat.

ON OCTOBER 15, DAN KELLEHER AND OTHER PERSONNEL FROM
the Office of Professional Discipline with the state department of education sat down with Dr. Andrew Reyner
to ask him about his relationship with Dean Faiello.
Reyner said that he and Dean were friends. He was also
sometimes a client of Dean's, who'd visited him for laser
hair removal.

He never mentioned that their "friendship" included
providing prescriptions and controlled substances to
Dean. He denied receiving any money from Dean or Skin-
Ovations, even though investigators had cancelled checks
in their possession written to Reyner and signed by Dean.
Dean's website named Reyner medical director of the
company, but Reyner insisted that the use of his name
was unauthorized, and that he had ordered Dean to remove his name from the web page. Reyner denied ever
writing any prescriptions for any of Dean's clients. He
said if they had any indication to the contrary, the only
possible explanation was that Dean stole prescription
pads from his office. Kelleher brought evidence of the
drug scripts; Reyner claimed the signatures on them were
forgeries.

Kelleher asked him to provide an exemplar of his signature. Reyner complied, deliberately distorting his handwriting in an attempt to disguise it and prove that it was not the same as the signature on the prescriptions.

The state department of education investigators doubted every word Reyner uttered. They were powerless, however, to take any action against a licensed physician. That authority was in the hands of the state department of health. They sent a report of their findings to that bureaucratic fortress for further investigation and possible disciplinary action.

IN THE MEANTIME, DEAN NEEDED MONEY—HIS FINANCIAL straits were desperate. That meant he needed to find work where he could earn a decent dollar for the time he spent on the job. It would be folly to think he could find employment doing electrolysis or laser under the supervision of another provider. There was only one answer in Dean's mind: continuing to see his clients. This determination did not die easy. Greg and other friends, concerned with his risky behavior, badgered Dean until they thought they convinced him it was not worth the price he would pay if he was discovered defying the orders of the court.

With no income, bankruptcy seemed inevitable. To forestall that possibility, Greg first contacted Dean's father, asking him if he would help Dean financially. Although Sam had the money to give Dean a fresh start, he refused. He'd helped him out before and gotten burned, he said. Next Greg went to Debra. "I'm not going bankrupt to help my brother," she told him. Still unaware that Dean's financial interactions with his family included ripping off his mother's estate, Greg was shocked by their coldness and unwillingness to help. He believed family members were supposed to help each other in times of crisis.

Greg set up an appointment with an accountant, who

met with the couple and devised a plan. Including the mortgage, Dean's debts approached half a million dollars. There was only one way to cut the financial burden down to size, the accountant said—sell off Dean's largest asset and the biggest source of indebtedness: the Newark house. With great reluctance, Dean agreed.

On the condition that Dean would not violate the court order, Greg agreed to support his lover until he went to jail. He kept Dean's mortgage current, paid utility bills and put food on the table. It was a crushing burden; Greg still had his own home to maintain and he'd used up much of his savings and incurred new debt helping Dean.

Greg agreed to this financial arrangement with the understanding that he would have Dean's power of attorney, should Dean be whisked off to jail. But Dean granted that authority to Debra. Wanting to remain in Dean's good graces, Greg shrugged that off. Debra was family, after all. He knew her and got along well with her. He had no reason to distrust her when she assured him that he would be reimbursed for all of his expenditures on Dean's behalf.

Greg had already invested so much in the Newark home; it seemed a better choice to give more with the possibility of recouping his expenditures than to just walk away from the money pit. Although Greg didn't think there was a place for him in Dean's future, he still loved the man. His goal was to liquidate Dean's assets, including the house, and create a nest egg that Dean could use to start his life over again when he left prison. He could not reach that goal unless the house sold for a decent price. Making that happen became a primary mission in Greg's life.

Dean may have accepted the reality of his situation, but that did not mean he could deal with it. He slid into a deep depression. He spent day and night in bed, with only occasional forays into the real world. Working out at the gym no longer held any attraction for him and the pounds piled on his previously svelte frame.

Dean no longer bothered to pull his mail out of the box. Greg assumed that responsibility and was shocked to discover the mountain of unpaid bills. It would be a miracle if they could hold their debtors at bay long enough to sell the house.

To make matters even worse, the house at 212 Elwood was not fit to go on sale. It needed repairs and a little polish to get a decent price. Greg despaired about the situation, but pulled money out of his pocket to make the home marketable. Dean did nothing but wallow in a slough of despondence and self-pity.

He pulled himself together enough to attend a neighborhood Halloween party, where he announced his need to sell the house and to spruce it up before putting it on the market. A neighbor introduced Dean to Dr. David Goldschmitt, director of the Emergency Services Department at NYU's Downtown Hospital, stating that Dean was a doctor. Dean did not contradict her.

The two men talked about how odd it was that they'd never met before. Their houses were just a block apart on opposite sides of the street. Dean arrived in the neighborhood nearly seventeen years earlier. David lived there for a decade longer than that.

The main topic of their conversation was the challenges presented by their two Victorian houses. David had finished his exterior work and planned to renovate the interior and turn his home into a showcase. Dean sought David's advice on the priorities for preparing his home for sale.

Soon after the party, Dean's neighbors came to the rescue in a more tangible way. A potluck supper morphed into a home improvement project. Neighbors spackled walls, painted trim, repaired cracks in the sidewalk and the basement walls and tackled problems in every corner of the house. Greg spent thousands of dollars out of his own pocket financing the repairs. He also prepared dinner every night for their battalion of helpers.

One of the more energetic supporters was Mark Ritchey, who lived a couple of blocks away. To Greg, Mark was a godsend. No one worked harder or spent longer hours laboring at the house night after night and weekend after weekend.

Mark had a neighborhood reputation for hyperbole and self-aggrandizement and his appearance was off-putting to some. His body was a walking tattoo parlor; his face reminded one neighbor of Satan himself. Greg passed the negative comments off as idle gossip. He thought that Mark worked on the house out of the goodness of his heart—that he volunteered his services as a good friend. Greg did not know that Dean was paying Mark for every minute of his time with the money Dean made from his surreptitious treatment of patients.

Dean put the house on the market with an asking price of $450,000. Thanks to the efforts of an energetic and determined neighborhood crew, Dean sold the house in record time for $423,000. They set a closing date for the spring. The buyer got a bargain—in 2005, county tax assessors valued the home at $496,600.

The buyer did not purchase the house without strings attached, though. A number of contingencies were placed on the sale. At lot of work needed to be done on the premises before the closing date.

Greg prepared to invest additional funds in the house to ensure that the sale would be finalized at the price stated. He wanted a guarantee, however, that he would be paid. He suggested that he put a lien on the house so that he would be the first debtor compensated after the bank loan balance was satisfied. Dean and Debra objected, convincing Greg that a lien could muck up the title transfer. Not wanting to cause any problems, he dropped that idea and obtained an attorney-drafted promissory note instead.

He did not know it at the time, but the mere suggestion of a lien angered Debra. He planted a seed of animosity and suspicion in Dean's sister's mind, one that would sprout into a major problem for Greg in the months to come.

WHILE GREG DUG HIMSELF A DEEPER HOLE, THE ATTORNEY general's office was doing the same for Dean. They worked at a fiery pace to solidify their case against the phony doctor. In addition to the evidence compiled by the three investigators from the state department of education, they had information gathered by their own investigators during the previous summer. They also had former patients of Dean's—including Sandra Corinthian, who suffered severe scarring from a tattoo removal—ready to testify against him.

They convened a special grand jury to review the charges in the case against Dean Faiello. On November 19, they issued a twenty-count indictment affirming the arraignment charges of three counts of assault in the second degree against Sandra Corinthian and seventeen counts of the unauthorized practice of medicine—one each for visits with undercover investigators Kathy Hearn, Tonya Holder and Ariana Miller and fourteen counts for his treatment of patient Jill Vasquez.

JASON OPSAHL'S CANCER RETURNED AGAIN—SHOWING UP soon after closing night for *The Full Monty*. He went into New York Weill Cornell Medical Center for his third brain surgery. His heart arrested during the procedure and Jason Opsahl died on October 25, 2002. Rosie O'Donnell, a friend to the end, flew to Florida. She sat with the family during the funeral service.

A distraught Broadway packed the John Houseman Theatre on 42nd Street on November 5 to bid farewell to the blonde actor with the baby face whom all the theater community had come to know and love. Technical show people assembled a moving media presentation of film footage and still shots. Among the attendees were Greg Bach and Dean Faiello.

Jerry Mitchell was there, too. In his twenty-five years in New York, he'd lost many friends to HIV/AIDS and was sorrowfully prepared for that eventuality. Now, though, he was devastated. He never thought he'd lose a good friend to cancer so young.

As he thought back on Jason, he remembered that when Jason was there with you, he was always totally present in the moment. "Jason taught me that quantity and quality are two completely different things," Jerry said. "None of us knows the quantity of time we will have, but we all can determine the quality."

Jason Opsahl was only 39 years old—the light of his talent, energy and generosity blinked out, no longer adding to the brilliance along the Great White Way.

Dean had no time to grieve the passing of his former lover. His own pile of problems continued to stack higher, threatening to bury him in an avalanche of self-created debris.

Missing poster for Maria Cruz.

Dean at Jason Opsahl's apartment on River Place. *Greg Bach*

Maria's apartment building on West 50th Street in New York. *Diane Fanning*

The building on West 16th Street where Dean had his last office. *Diane Fanning*

Laser machine used by Dean Faiello. *Greg Bach*

The carriage house where Maria's body was buried. *Diane Fanning*

Carmel, Dean, and Debra Faiello. *Greg Bach*

Greg Bach posed with his sand sculpture. *Greg Bach*

Greg Bach and Dean Faiello in a friend's garden. *Greg Bach*

Exterior of 212 Elwood. *Greg Bach*

Living room and sitting room at 212 Elwood. *Greg Bach*

In Celebration of the Life of

JASON OPSAHL

Tuesday, November 5, 2002

Program for Jason Opsahl's memorial service. *Greg Bach*

St. Malachy's—The Actors' Chapel. *Diane Fanning*

Dean Faiello relaxing on vacation. *Greg Bach*

CHAPTER NINETEEN

FINALLY, DEAN GOT A COUPLE OF PIECES OF GOOD NEWS. HIS lawyer, Margaret Shalley, worked a deal with Ronda Lustman at the attorney general's office. It meant that Dean would only have to spend a maximum of 6 months in jail. To get this lenient sentence, he first had to cooperate with authorities in their investigation of a handful of physicians.

The second stroke of luck came when he heard he would inherit some money. When Jason Opsahl died in surgery, Dean was still listed as the beneficiary of what was once a small pension account Jason maintained through the Actor's Guild. By 2002, the value of that account approached $100,000.

Although Jason never followed through with the official paperwork, he made it clear in writing that he wanted his brothers' children to inherit his pension. Jason's brother Bart called Dean to discuss it. "Look," he said, "you and I both know it wasn't Jason's wish for you to have all that money. Jason wanted it for his nieces and nephews. You are entitled to some of it, but the rest should go to the kids."

Dean agreed on all points. He said he would look over the paperwork, figure out what needed to be done to make that happen and would get back to Bart. Bart was pleased by Dean's surprisingly agreeable attitude.

But Dean never called. Instead, he complained to Greg about his difficulty in getting his rightful inheritance. He did not mention his conversation with Bart, and Greg, knowing only part of the story, offered up the money for Dean to hire another attorney for advice on the matter.

IN THE FALL OF 2002, TOM SHANAHAN'S LAW FIRM WAS ONLY three years old. His practice focused on employment-related discrimination law affecting the gay, lesbian, bisexual and trans-gendered communities. With every passing day, though, he was gaining prominence as an openly gay attorney with a willingness to represent community organizations and not-for-profits in *pro bono* litigation. He ran his practice on the belief that "even unpopular litigants have a right to their day in court and even unpopular litigants have a right to counsel."

Shanahan represented the families of twenty 9–11 victims, two members of Congress, numerous community groups and the New York City Uniformed Fire Officers Association in a case that sought to compel the Port Authority to reconstruct the World Trade Center in conformance with the New York City building and fire codes. He challenged the religious exemption to the New Jersey Law Against Discrimination when he stood up for gay and lesbian students who were denied the opportunity to form a student organization at Seton Hall University. Shanahan obtained a successful judgment in the first ever jury trial of a transsexual fired under New York's administrative code. He was successful in one of the first same-sex visitation cases, involving the non-biological mother's right to see her child after ending a relationship with her lesbian partner.

In a case that demonstrated his creativity and sense of

humor, Shanahan joined a team of volunteer lawyers to save *New York* magazine–rated "Best Dive Bar," Siberia. Their client alleged that the landlord, Mitsubishi, harassed the bar in an attempt to evict—going so far as to rip a toilet from the wall and cause flooding. Shanahan, along with Siberia's owner Tracy Westmoreland, traveled to Tokyo and chained themselves to the toilet in front of Mitsubishi world headquarters.

Tom's beginnings were truly humble. His father was raised in Jersey City by working-class Irish-Catholic immigrants. His Iranian mother emigrated from Tehran to work as a nurse at the Roosevelt Hospital in Manhattan. They met while ballroom dancing at the Roseland, started their married life in Hell's Kitchen, then moved to Staten Island, where Tom grew up.

To pay his way through New York Law School, Shanahan worked full-time and part-time for five years for New York's first public advocate, Mark Green. Then he joined Tratner & Molloy, a New York law firm, where he litigated discrimination cases, ultimately establishing his own firm, Shanahan & Associates, in 1999.

Although Tom was not as prominent in 2002 when Greg and Dean came to his door, it was clear that Greg Bach had not selected a lightweight to represent his lover. At Shanahan's direction, Dean sent a letter to Bart indicating that he was legally entitled to the inheritance, and that he intended to keep it. When he accepted the civil case on Dean's behalf, Shanahan had no awareness of his client's current travails with the attorney general's office.

But Dean hit another glitch: The pension fund managers wanted written assurance that Jason had no children. No matter who was listed as beneficiary, the distribution was set up so that the money automatically went to any of Jason's offspring—if he had any. If not, they needed a signed document to this effect from Jason's family.

The company sent forms to Jason's brother Bart in Florida. Bart was reluctant to sign—he did not think his brother had any children, but didn't know for sure. Dean badgered him to sign the paperwork, even offering to split the money with him. Bart still balked—he did not want to make a statement that might be fraudulent, and he was more than a little annoyed with Dean's prickly behavior. He still felt that, although Dean should be repaid for the loan, the bulk of the funds belonged to Jason's nephews.

ON DECEMBER 6, 2002, DEAN APPEARED IN COURT WITH HIS AT-torney Margaret Shalley. In keeping with the plea agreement Shalley crafted that limited his jail time to 6 months, he pled guilty to seventeen misdemeanor counts and not guilty to the three felony counts, all connected to the indictment handed down by the grand jury in November.

DEAN'S PLEA-BARGAINED SHORTER SENTENCE, HIS HOUSE SALE and his possible inheritance windfall all relieved Greg tremendously. It looked to Greg as if he'd accomplished his goal to get all of Dean's affairs in order before he served time behind bars. After Dean paid the bank and other creditors and reimbursed Greg, he would still have a $150,000 nest egg when he was released after a short 6-month stay in jail. Greg was impressed with Margaret Shalley and appreciative of her work. Reducing a 4-year sentence to half a year seemed like a miracle.

Greg worked to create a light and happy atmosphere for Dean, especially since the reality of Dean's life was now so dark—so tragically sad. Greg decorated the Newark house inside and out for the holidays. He threw a Christmas party that looked lavish, though it was planned on a shoe-string budget. As an experienced event planner, Greg was a master at creating extravagance at a very low cost.

And the money Greg disbursed seemed well spent. It

provided a showcase for the estate sale coming up in January, it was a nice way to say goodbye to a house that held so many memories, and it gave Dean a memorable send-off before beginning his jail sentence.

Despite all this, Dean's spirits remained low. For him, those impending 6 months in jail might as well have been 6 years, or even 60. The thought of any time behind bars terrified him. Through email, he resumed contact with Chris Buczek, a boyfriend from two decades earlier. In his messages, he often rambled about the anxiety he felt over spending time in jail.

Dean's apathy continued to drive Greg to distraction. While Dean slept or lounged about, Greg went off to work. Although he had time on his hands, Dean wouldn't lift a finger around the house. One day, for instance, Dean promised to install new press-on tiles for the kitchen floor. When Greg returned to Newark after work, not one new tile was in place.

Greg was frustrated. He worked hard to support Dean and finance the renovations and repairs on the home that was required for the sale. He also gave Dean pocket money, though taking care never to give him too much at one time—if he did, he feared Dean would blow it all on drugs.

A long-time friend of Dean's, Patty Rosado, visited him often after his arrest. She tried to take his mind off of his troubles with *Six Feet Under*, *Sex and the City* and other DVDs, which they sometimes watched together until dawn.

One day, Patty sarcastically told Greg, "Don't give him any more money. He's got money of his own now." They both suspected that Dean had reopened Skin-Ovations and was treating people with a laser again. When Patty later learned that Dean paid a lot of money to friend Carl James for use of his apartment at 151 16th Street, they were sure of it.

Greg was perplexed. He provided for all of Dean's needs. *Why would Dean need more money?*

Greg contacted Margaret Shalley and shared his suspicions with her. She said there was nothing she could do but warn Dean of the consequences of violating the court order. That warning had no impact on Dean's actions, prompting Patty to confront him. Dean lashed out, offended by the invasion of his privacy. What Dean in fact wanted was something Greg would not provide—drugs. Now that Andrew Reyner and doctor of osteopathy Michael Jackowitz were being grilled about Dean's prescriptions for Stadol and other drugs, he no longer had access to his pharmaceutical highs. Now any drug would do. He was buying whatever was available from an assortment of street dealers. And to get that money, he needed to get back to work.

One of his new patients came to him for laser treatments for a condition called black hairy tongue. Her name was Maria Cruz.

DEAN'S FIRST CONFERENCE AS PART OF HIS PLEA AGREEMENT was in March 2003. He and his attorney entered a conference room filled with representatives of the office of the attorney general, the department of education and the department of health.

He admitted to them that he had in fact introduced himself to patients as Dr. Faiello. They wanted information on the doctors who supplied him with prescription drugs. "Are you selling these painkillers to others?"

"No," Dean said. "I'm a Stadol addict. I want it all for myself."

Dean provided authorities with emails and cancelled checks incriminating Dr. Andrew Reyner, a Manhattan psychopharmacologist; Michael Jackowitz, a doctor of osteopathy; and other physicians. Authorities suspected both Réyner and Jackowitz of supplying Dean with anesthesia, prescriptions and pills. Reyner had at one time been listed as a laser specialist on the SkinOvation website.

When questioned later through his attorney, Reyner denied having had contact with Dean since February 2001, when he wrote a letter asking that his name be removed from the website. Dean had once been a patient, nothing more, Reyner claimed.

Dean left the meeting, still free on bail while awaiting sentencing, promising that he would return with any additional information he could find.

MARCH 9, 2003, WAS MARIA CRUZ'S 35TH BIRTHDAY. HER BROTHER Jun called her from the Philippines to wish her a wonderful day. They talked and laughed, both of them looking forward to Jun's planned trip to New York a little more than a month away. That day, Jun had no idea that he would never hear his sister's voice again.

CHAPTER TWENTY

COMPOSER STEPHEN SCHWARTZ STEPPED INTO DEAN'S LIFE that spring. Stephen was a New York City native, born there in 1948. He studied at the Juilliard School of Music while in high school and graduated with a B.F.A. from Carnegie Mellon University in 1968.

A true Broadway luminary, Schwartz started his career as a producer for RCA Records and earned his first major Broadway credit when he wrote the title song for *Butterflies Are Free*. In 1971, he won two Grammys for the music and lyrics to *Godspell*. He also won acclaim as a director, capturing the Drama Desk Award for a musical version of Studs Terkel's *Working*, which he also co-directed for television. He composed scores for full-length animated features as well, racking up three Academy Awards and another Grammy.

When he started seeing Dean Faiello, Stephen was working on the music for a Broadway production. *Wicked*, a musical prequel to *The Wizard of Oz*, was a tale about the college years of the wicked witch Elphaba and the good witch Glinda. It was scheduled to open in the fall of that year.

Greg was aware of Stephen and knew that he and Dean were friends. He even had dinner with them one evening. Dean was clearly impressed with Stephen and chattered to Greg about their social encounters, describing a dinner where other guests included Meryl Streep and Kevin Kline.

That Dean would have a friendship with someone of Stephen's prominence did not surprise Greg. Dean had always attracted smart, successful people. But Greg was shocked when Patty Rosado told him the truth: Dean and Stephen were involved in what one gossip columnist called "a torrid affair."

Before Dean's arrest in October 2002, Patty worked part-time on Saturdays as Dean's receptionist. Dean eventually had to produce a massive amount of documentation to the attorney general's office to satisfy the conditions of his plea bargain, and Patty volunteered to get his financial records and client files in order.

Sometimes she worked late into the night—occasionally all night—to meet the deadlines. Patty had a natural knack for this kind of work, and incredible organizational skills. Without her help, Dean might have blown the whole deal.

Unbeknownst to Dean, Patty was taking advantage of her access to Dean's computers to hack into his email and spy on him. It was how she learned of Dean's arrangements to use Carl James' apartment, in late 2002. And it was how she stumbled across a passionate declaration of love from Stephen Schwartz that spring.

Patty forwarded that email to Greg. She said that as a friend, she felt obligated to let Greg know what was happening. At the time, Greg accepted that explanation of her good intentions. Nonetheless, he chastised her for violating Dean's privacy.

NOT LONG AFTER HER BIRTHDAY, MARIA CRUZ EMAILED DEAN Faiello. She complained of nausea and dizziness in the aftermath of her last laser treatment. Dean recommended over-the-counter remedies. Her next appointment was scheduled for Friday, April 11, though obligations at the office forced her to postpone. Dean agreed to see her on Sunday evening, April 13. It pleased the work-centric Maria that Dean could accommodate her outside of regular business hours. Her position at Barclays was demanding, and she was trusted with multi-million-dollar decisions. Although beguiled and duped by Dean's false credentials and smooth bedside manner, Maria was, ironically, a specialist in researching health care companies.

Dean emailed her before that Sunday visit. "I have to pick up lidocaine and syringes. Could you please pay in cash instead of a check?"

Maria did not express any concern about this unorthodox request. With her intelligence and business savvy, Maria was one of the last people anyone would suspect of being vulnerable to a quack's con. But she accepted everything as unvarnished truth from this man she believed to be a physician.

After a day of attending mass, doing prep work for a meeting the next day, running errands—including the withdrawal of $400 cash from an ATM—Maria traveled down to the Chelsea area of Manhattan. She stopped to shop at Loehmann's, then entered the building at 151 West 16th Street for her appointment with Dean Faiello.

The condition requiring treatment, black tongue, was minor and temporary—often brought on by diet or medication. Usually, a doctor would give patients like Maria a series of tongue scrapings in his office and recommend vigorous toothbrushing on the surface of the tongue at home, in between visits.

Maria had opted for laser treatment because she found it less painful than scraping. But in choosing Dean Faiello, she ran a grave risk. The problem with her tongue was mild, and a true physician would have recognized the difference between the minor black tongue ailment she suffered and the far more serious one of hairy leukoplakia—a precancerous overgrowth of the cilia. Had she suffered the latter, Dean's treatment might have only concealed the symptoms, as the cancer continued to flourish undetected.

On April 13, nothing seemed out of the ordinary until Maria's body began rocking with convulsions, following an injection of lidocaine into her tongue. Dean consulted a physician but did not get the advice he wanted. Dr. Goldschmitt told him that the only hope Maria had for survival would be her immediate transport to the emergency room.

Dean decided not to take this advice. He knew his plea bargain and his freedom would disappear if it was discovered that he was still treating patients. There would be an immediate arrest and incarceration without bail for the maximum sentence of 4 years.

Not willing to make that sacrifice, Dean gambled with Maria's life. He waited, hoping that she would pull out of the convulsions on her own. It was a selfish wager—one destined for failure. Maria Cruz died at 8 P.M. on April 13, 2003.

Again, Dean Faiello faced a decision. Should he do the right thing and call the police? Or should he, once more, seek a solution to protect himself?

Dean chose the latter. He allowed his anxiety about life in prison to outweigh the value of decency toward another human being. If he thought about the worry he would cause Maria's family and friends if she disappeared into thin air, he pushed that concern out of his head. Foremost in his mind was his desire to save himself.

After years of pushing closer and closer to the edge—of blurring the legal and ethical distinctions between right and wrong—he fell off the precipice, past the point of no return. His arrogance, lust for control and sense of being above the law drove his every choice. And when it came down to a decision between what was best for him and what was best for Maria—whether it was worth risking an innocent person to save himself—he acted in his own best interests.

Compounding the horror of what he had already done, he treated Maria like soiled laundry, stuffing her into a suitcase and lugging her home.

CHAPTER TWENTY-ONE

TES LARA AND JUN CRUZ, FAR FROM THEIR HOMES IN THE Philippines, staggered under the weight of their sister Maria's disappearance. Her New York and New Jersey family members rallied around them to help find Maria and bring her home. They reported her missing, enlisting the investigative skills of Detective Joe Della Rocca.

They called television, radio and newspaper journalists, trying stir up interest in Maria's story and inform the public. They posted 200 fliers a day in Manhattan, Queens, Jersey City and elsewhere. The poster read:

> Her disappearance is a complete mystery, baffling us all.
> If anyone has seen [Maria Cruz] or has any information
> about her whereabouts, the police and the family would
> like to hear from you.
>
> —Jun Cruz, a brother of Maria.

Uncle Jose picked a different avenue of New York each time he went out. He walked its length from Upper Manhattan to deep into downtown, putting up posters on every block.

They launched a website, www.mariacruzmissing.com, and posted letters about her disappearance all over the Internet. Sheila Samonte-Pescayo, cousin and columnist in

the Philippines and in California, used her media access
to issue a personal appeal on the one-month anniversary
of Maria's disappearance, pleading for help and prayers:

> Maria, whom we fondly call "Ate Pipay," was on the top
> of her career, being the senior financial analyst at Bar-
> clays Bank, one of the biggest in the Big Apple, which
> pays her a salary of $180,000 a year. Her baffling case
> has drawn the interest of Wall Street and many New
> Yorkers. In one telecast, Fox News television station
> regarded her disappearing act more important than
> Madonna's performance in a West End play.

Her sister Tes told *48 Hours*: "My sister was six years
younger than I, but she was like a big sister. My sister was
very gutsy. She was a big dreamer. When she told me she
wanted to go to the U.S., there was no other way for me
but to encourage her to go on and fulfill her dreams." Her
disappearance, she said, "left this big gaping hole in my
heart. From the very start, I knew something very wrong
had happened to her. It was terrible. It felt like the world
had just caved in on me."

All across the country, devastated families understood
her pain. They retained a sliver of hope that Maria would
return unharmed. They hung in agonizing limbo. Until
the discovery of a body, their minds raced with endless,
trepidatious questions.

Maria's family maintained a command center for the
search. Every day, someone picked up the phone and
called the police. The NYPD was not idle—they devoted
significant resources to the search. Wally Zeins, commanding officer of the Manhattan Detectives Nightwatch
in 2003, told *48 Hours* that investigators were suspicious
from the start: "Maria Cruz had a very normal life. We
knew she was religious. We knew she would work on her

day off. And then everything changed. She was here to-day, vanished tomorrow. A lot of things led detectives to believe there was foul play somewhere along the line."

In June, authorities in New Jersey discovered a small-statured Asian woman who'd been beaten, mugged and left for dead. The New Jersey medical center called the Cruz family to come view the body for identification.

Jun stood outside the hospital, unable to cross the threshold. His limbs shook, his breath was shortened. He shivered in the street, even in the pounding heat of the Jersey sun. Uncle Jose took the lead, and to his great relief, it was not the body of his missing niece. Hope flared bright, the nightmares suppressed for one more day.

CHAPTER TWENTY-TWO

IMMEDIATELY AFTER MARIA'S DEATH, DEAN ENLISTED THE help of his friends Patty Rosado and Mark Ritchey to change the locks on the doors of his home and on the wrought-iron gates surrounding it. Dean told Mark that he wanted to discourage trespassers and to keep Greg out of the house—Dean was tired of all his whining.

Mark and Patty claim they did not know about the more urgent, darker reason Dean wanted to keep Greg and others out. Greg, too, had no clue about the macabre truth that was now hidden at 212 Elwood. He was also unaware of his own banishment. Arriving at Dean's house to help with the cleanup and repair chores, he pulled on the gate. It was locked. He pulled out his key. It didn't fit.

Greg was enraged.

He climbed up a tree next to the fence and eased himself down into the yard. The fencing cut into his hands, scraped up his arms, ripped his pants and scratched his legs. He approached the house and discovered, again, that the doors were locked and the locks were changed.

After all Greg had done for Dean, after all of Dean's professions of love, Greg was furious and hurt that Dean would play these passive-aggressive games with him. He grabbed a ladder from the yard and propped it up against a balcony. Climbing into the house, he headed straight for Dean's bedroom. That door was locked, too. Greg flipped. He lifted his leg waist-high and slammed it into the knob of the shut door. It flew open.

A drowsy Dean sat in stunned silence as Greg stood at the foot of the bed ranting. Still fuming, Greg walked out of the room and picked up the telephone. He called Patty at work and told her about the locks. "Did you know he was going to do this?" Greg asked.

"I did know about it, Greg, but I told Dean and Mark that they needed to tell you before you came all the way out here and couldn't get in."

"Well, actually, I could and I did get in," Greg said.

"Are you there now?"

"Yes."

"Now, technically, you are trespassing," Patty said, leaving an unspoken threat hanging in the air.

"Okay, fine. I'm trespassing. Call the police. I'll sit on the front porch and read a magazine and wait until they get here. I know where Dean hid all the drugs and I'll be glad to show them," Greg said.

Greg didn't sit and wait, though. He had a serious need for empathy. He walked down the street to the home of a neighbor he knew well. The man's partner was out of the country on an extended trip and, in all likelihood, would welcome some company. The visit was just what Greg needed. A couple of hours later, in a far calmer state, he returned to Dean's house, but Dean was nowhere to be found. Greg made himself comfortable and awaited his return.

Greg was deeply hurt by Dean's behavior and a bit perturbed at Mark and Patty's willingness to participate in the conspiracy to lock him out of the house. He hoped that he and Dean could talk out the problem that evening.

But Dean did not come home alone. He arrived with Mark and Patty, who were markedly hostile. Greg had noticed that the attitudes of those two toward him had deteriorated in recent weeks. It took the conversation that night to help him understand why. Dean had systematically poisoned their well of sympathy by vilifying Greg—Patty was even convinced that Greg was taking advantage of Dean's financial difficulties to turn a profit for himself.

There was one more reason for Patty's growing antipathy, one that would remain hidden from him for three more months.

But Greg assumed there was only one reason for Dean to make him look bad. Dean planned to break up with him and wanted to justify that action to himself and to his friends. As far as Greg knew, there was only one thing to hide—the drugs. He had no suspicion that Dean had a dead body in his possession. Looking back, he now believes that night must have been the night Dean moved the body from the carriage house to Mark's garage.

Mark claimed he had no knowledge of Maria's death, but in hindsight, he suspected that Dean had kept the body of Maria Cruz in his garage on Highland Street along with other possessions, stored in preparation for his move. There was a foul odor in May, but Mark thought his Great Dane had dragged in a dead squirrel. It sounded implausible, but with one glance into Mark's garage—packed so tight, it was impossible to enter—the idea suddenly seemed credible.

Even after Dean's conspiring, Greg did not abandon him. He'd made a promise to see Dean's problems through to the end, and he intended to keep his commitment, continuing to play an active role in readying the home for sale.

On Saturday, May 24, Greg planned a garage sale of everything that had not been sold at the estate sale or on eBay. A number of articles of value remained, including a large Chinese vase. One neighbor brought over a few things of his own to sell. He and his little dog Lulu spent the whole day with Greg, rather than leave him minding the makeshift store alone.

Greg expected Dean to help out with the sale, and again, Dean disappointed him. Not only did he stay in the house, he wouldn't even get out of bed. Not once during that long day did Greg notice any unusual odors in the garage. Even Lulu, with her sharpened sense of smell, never expressed any interest in the garage's contents.

At midnight that night, Patty called Greg, accusing him of stealing Dean's grandmother's parfait glasses. She claimed that Dean promised them to her. Greg couldn't believe what he was hearing. The glasses had little value. "If I were going to steal something," he told her, "I would have taken something of value, like his grandmother's sterling flatware."

"So, did you steal that, too?"

Greg hung up the phone, exasperated. He'd gone to great pains to make sure that flatware got to Debra. The more he thought about it the angrier he got. He fired off a nasty email to Patty, a cruel, insensitive message he regretted seconds after he hit "send."

Greg was still sitting at Dean's desk when an email popped up in the mailbox. It was from Patty. She had forwarded Greg's ranting, hate-filled email to Dean and Debra. "See, I told you Greg was nuts," she wrote. Greg deleted the message from Dean's computer, but there was nothing he could do about Debra. He knew he'd blown it. His relationship with her was destroyed.

BUT GREG WAS STILL THERE FOR DEAN, STICKING IT OUT TO THE bitter end. He still planned on letting Dean stay at his apartment until he had to go off to jail, even though Greg knew their relationship was over. On May 27, the day before the house closing, Patty hinted that Dean had a different plan—he was moving into Mark's place. Greg confronted Mark about it.

"I have no idea," Mark claimed. "You'll have to ask Dean."

But Greg didn't bother—he no longer cared. Mark's house was in the neighborhood. The move there would be less disruptive. Living at Mark's house might be the best solution after all.

TUESDAY WHIRLED BY, AND THE ACTIVITY AT 212 ELWOOD grew frenzied. Greg hauled trash and loaded his belongings into a rented Jeep. Inside the garage and out, he thought he smelled something rotting; but, like Mark before him, he assumed it was a squirrel, rat or raccoon lying dead in a remote corner. He didn't give it much thought. He also paid little attention to Dean's project in the garage—until he'd been at it for quite a while. Greg finally asked Dean what he was doing with all that cement, but he didn't get a straight answer. Greg shrugged it off, unaware that he was witnessing the burial of Maria Cruz in a sloppy, cold concrete vault.

Greg's original plan was to go home to Manhattan that evening. He wanted to return the Jeep first thing in the morning to avoid additional rental charges. Looking around at all that remained to do, he decided to stay longer—overnight if necessary. Besides, he'd been so busy taking care of chores for Dean, he hadn't had a chance to pack up his own clothing.

Greg was occupied in the kitchen fixing dinner when Mark and Patty showed up. The pistachioes he'd snacked on all day were now just a bag of shells. Dean snatched it up off the counter by the wrong end and sent shells clattering across the floor. "Pick them up," Dean yelled at Greg.

Patty and Mark chimed in, too, ganging up on him.

After spouting a few words of pent-up venom, Greg gathered up his clothes and stormed out of the house, never to return. His relationship with Dean was over.

Dean gathered the few things that hadn't already been stuffed in boxes, packed them up and moved into the third floor of Mark's home just a couple blocks away.

Greg did not hear from Dean again for three long days—three days in which he hung in anxiety. He felt his future hinging on Dean and whether Dean would pay back the money Greg invested in the house. Three days wondering if Dean was capable of doing the right thing.

CHAPTER TWENTY-THREE

AT LAST, DEAN CALLED GREG. AT THE SOUND OF DEAN'S voice, Greg's heart filled with joy and his mind with turmoil. He knew Dean had treated him badly. He knew their romantic relationship was over. But still Dean stirred him. They had a pleasant conversation and Greg invited him to come into the city, offering to treat him to dinner at a nearby Indian restaurant. Over their meal, the two talked about bringing their relationship to an amiable close. Dean apologized for not telling him that he planned to move in with Mark. It was just easier, he reasoned. "I didn't want to tell because I didn't want to hurt your feelings."

Greg accepted his apology and Dean stayed the night at Greg's. They parted the next day, expressing a mutual desire to remain friends. Although they talked on the phone several times in the coming months, they never again saw each other face-to-face that summer.

THEIR NEXT PHONE CONVERSATION STARTED OUT FINE, BUT turned into an argument. "I've been thinking of going to Italy," Dean announced. The terms of his bond permitted leaving the country as long as he returned for any court dates.

"That would be wonderful for you. You've never been to Italy," Greg said. "You ought to go and enjoy a vacation before you go to jail. But before you do, pay me the money you owe me first."

Dean blasted Greg for always thinking of himself, then promptly hung up.

ON JUNE 26, 2003, DEAN RETURNED TO COURT TO PLEAD GUILTY to the three felony counts related to his arrest for practicing medicine without a license. His sentencing date was set for September 5.

MEANWHILE, DEBRA HAD BEGUN HANDLING A LOT OF DEAN'S financial affairs. As soon as the sale of the house was final, she sent Greg a check for $10,000, an amount that covered only a portion of his expenditures on Dean's behalf. He was still owed another $85,000 for the cash he shelled out on Dean's mortgage payments, legal costs, living expenses and home repairs. Dean made excuses for not paying Greg, claiming that he wanted to, but couldn't at that moment.

Debra questioned every penny that Greg requested. Despite her previous promises, she now expressed certainty that Greg was not entitled to reimbursement for all the expenses he claimed. She took particular umbrage at Greg's request for repayment of money he shelled out in supporting Dean for nine months, demanding an itemized list. She insisted that every expense be backed with a receipt. Greg had not expected that documentation would be required and so did not keep an organized file. It took him weeks to get it together, and when he turned it over to Debra, he expected to be paid. Instead, Debra sent the packet of material off to an attorney.

THE NEXT MONTH, DEAN CALLED GREG, WHINING ABOUT Patty. "I can't get her out of my life. What can I do?"

At first, Greg did not comprehend the depth of Dean's

problem. He made a few suggestions, which Dean dismissed out of hand.

"What's the real problem, Dean?"

He spelled it out in crude terms: Dean had had sex with Patty on more than one occasion. Patty had done so much for him, he explained, and that was how she'd wanted Dean to pay her back.

You mean that's how you were able to take advantage of her for so long, Greg thought. Suddenly, it all made sense. Much of what Patty had done and said took on a different cast. Patty was hostile to Greg because she was jealous; she'd wanted Dean as her boyfriend. She saw herself as an exception—the one woman who could captivate and capture the handsome gay guy—and she wanted to keep him for her own.

Greg now understood: Patty hadn't told him about Dean's affair with Stephen Schwartz out of friendship. She did it because she wanted to drive Greg out of Dean's life. She didn't stay up all night getting documents ready for Dean's attorney out of the unbridled goodness of her heart. She did it to weave a web of need around Dean, and to draw him away from Greg.

Greg couldn't be angry at Patty—now, he only felt sorry for her. She had put herself in a position to be used and tossed aside, and that was just what was happening to her now. As he ended the conversation, Greg could barely keep the disgust out of his voice.

DEAN CALLED GREG AGAIN IN MID-SUMMER TO TELL HIM about a vision he'd had. "I was driving down a road and had to stop because a mother deer and her two baby deer were crossing the road," he said. "While I waited, I had a vision of my mother standing in the road. She had a sad expression on her face. I realized then how disappointed she would be if she knew you and Debra were fighting about money." Dean paused, expecting a sympathetic response. Greg had always been a soft touch whenever Dean evoked his mother.

Greg, however, was not swayed by Dean's bald attempt at manipulation. *This is just more of Dean's crap*, Greg thought. *And I'm sick of listening to it.* This time, it was Greg who hung up the phone.

BY LATE AUGUST, GREG WAS FED UP. HE CALLED DEBRA AND explained his current economic hardship and his need for repayment. She said, "I would not have done what you did with Dean. You got yourself into this mess; you can get yourself out of it."

In anger, Greg called Dean. "If you're gonna fuck me over on this, I'm gonna fuck you over back."

"No, you're not," Dean said. "You're not that type."

Ashamed, Greg knew Dean was right.

"What are you going to do, Greg?" Dean taunted. Greg still did not respond, and Dean laughed at him. He considered threatening to report Dean for still seeing clients, but before he could, Dean hung up.

At the same time, Dean was also driving Mark crazy. He slept all day, snorted cocaine all night. He never remembered to lock the door, and he shamelessly rifled through Mark's belongings—even borrowing Mark's clothing. Dean cranked up the air conditioning on high all day while Mark worked in Manhattan as a hair stylist. That drove Mark's electricity bill up close to $500 for the month of July alone. Mark told him to stop, even wrote notes ordering it, but Dean persisted.

Mark tried talking to his boarder, but Dean would not change. In addition to his annoying and costly habits, Mark was concerned that he might be arrested if Dean was caught in his house with drugs. He ordered Dean out in mid-August. Dean took refuge in Patty Rosado's home.

Soon thereafter, Mark spent an afternoon out in the garage shifting around the belongings Dean had left behind for storage. He wanted to fit them all into a tighter space in order to have a pathway through the garage.

In the process, he picked up a piece of luggage. Lifting it onto a stack of boxes, he heard something move around inside. Mark set down the pack, unzipped it and found a woman's purse. It contained tampons and an address book, along with credit cards and a driver's license belonging to someone named Maria Cruz.

He pulled his cell phone out of his pocket and picked a number at random from the address book. It rang and rang but no one ever answered. He tried another number but no one picked up there either. On the third call, he got an answer.

"Do you know Maria Cruz?" Mark asked.

He was told he had the wrong number.

Mark decided he didn't want to know why Maria Cruz's purse was in Dean's things. He put it back in the suitcase and added it to the top of a stack of boxes against the wall. He never mentioned his discovery to Dean.

ONE NIGHT IN LATE AUGUST, DEAN DROVE UP TO BELLEVILLE, looking for a home to buy. A neighbor spotted him peering into the windows of one house and called the police. When they responded, Dean could not produce a license, registration or proof of insurance. The police found something in his car, though: cocaine. They hauled him to jail, where Patty came to bail him out.

In no time, Dean wore out his welcome at Patty's place. He moved into a motel in Secaucus.

On September 5, Dean was due in court. He didn't show. His attorney did not know where he was, and the bail bondsman could not find him. The attorney general's office threatened to revoke his plea agreement.

Five days later, Dean visited his safe-deposit box at Wachovia bank. He removed the cash he'd been stashing there since Maria's death.

Two weeks later, Mark Ritchey discovered a message in his voicemail intended for Dean. It was an airline courtesy call confirming his reservation that day. Dean boarded a Continental flight bound for Costa Rica with a three-month visa.

Within days, Greg got a call from Dean's former housekeeper, Elizabeth. She told him that a hysterical Patty Rosado had telephoned. Sobbing, she'd told Elizabeth, "Dean's left the country and he's never coming back."

A few hours later, the bail company called Greg. They wanted to know where Dean was, and Greg told them what he knew. They informed him that if Dean did not show for his next court appearance, Greg, as the person who originally posted bail, would have to come up with the rest of the money.

CHAPTER TWENTY-FOUR

THE SUN GLISTENED OFF THE AIRCRAFT AND THE ASTONISH-
ing blues of the Caribbean Sea as the Continental flight
approached Costa Rica. Lazy waves splashed against im-
maculate black and white sand beaches, the plane passing
them and moving inland. Intense emerald green vistas
soon emerged.

Costa Rica possesses as many species of plant life as
all of Europe. From his window, Dean could view dense
forest canopies and rugged mountains. Four volcanoes—
two of them active—thrust into the sky near the plane's
destination. It had been forty years since the last eruption
brought devastation to the people of Costa Rica—the
danger, though now dormant, remained quite alive.

Wheels touched down, bouncing off the tarmac of
Juan Santamaria Airport in San Jose, a city four thousand
feet above sea level. Dean had successfully left his home
country—where the body of Maria Cruz lay encased in
concrete.

BORDERED BY NICARAGUA AND PANAMA TO THE NORTH AND
south and by the Caribbean Sea and the Pacific Ocean to
the east and west, Costa Rica is a land of lush jungles filled
with the shrieks and antics of monkeys, the threat of crocodiles, jungle cats and poison dart frogs, the hypnotizing

slow-motion movement of three-toed sloths and a mind-boggling assortment of lizards, exotic birds and butter-flies. On both coasts, endangered sea turtles nest.

All of these natural wonders and a population of four million are contained in a nation not quite the size of West Virginia. Unlike its neighbors, Costa Rica is a stable entity—only two brief periods of violence rocked its history since the late nineteenth century.

Although its culture is far different from what Dean had known all his life, Costa Rica's class structure felt a lot like home. The government made a marked impact on the lives of its poorer citizens—reducing poverty and constructing a strong social safety net, creating the largest middle class in Central America—a population far more upwardly mobile than any of the other nations in the area.

Racially, Dean fit right in, too. Ninety per cent of the citizens are whites of Spanish origin with a mixture of German, Italian, English and other European nationalities, making this country the most homogenized population in the region. Adding to the gringo cast of the country, about a quarter of a million full-time residents of Coast Rica are foreigners—mostly Americans and Canadians.

Despite these influences, the culture of Costa Rica remains very Latin—Catholicism dominates and the extended family is the basis for social life.

DEAN LANDED IN A CITY WHERE SPRING IS ALWAYS IN THE AIR. The average year-round temperature is 74 degrees—a radical departure from New Jersey and New York. He arrived in the middle of the rainy season, when most of the day is sunny but the early afternoon is marked by an hour or two of intense rain.

More than the weather separated the residents of Dean's new home from his native country. He faced a new world where the language of the masses was Spanish.

Although Costa Ricans were known for their patience with non–Spanish speaking visitors, it nonetheless presented a barrier for Dean.

There was a marked difference in the lifestyle of the people. The pace slowed dramatically. To Dean, who lived in the orbit of a major urban center all his life, it appeared as if there was no evidence of planning in daily life—as if to-do lists were an alien concept.

Long lines were a common experience in San Jose, Costa Rica's capital since 1823. Josefinos waited at banks, telephone offices, post offices, nearly everywhere. They accepted this inconvenience and treated it as a social opportunity. This tendency drove Dean to distraction—like most Americans, he did not possess an abundance of patience.

Dean emerged from his flight, passed through customs and hailed an official orange airport taxi for the ride to his hotel. He'd just set foot in San Jose, the only over-populated area in the country—70 percent of the nation's people resided in the city and its surrounding metropolitan area.

For a homosexual male like Dean, there appeared at first glance to be an innate conflict between his sexual preference and the people of Costa Rica, who, as a rule, clung to conservative family values and traditional gender roles. Machismo reigned—men and women were expected to behave differently and conform to the parameters of the gender of their birth. Women achieved success in business and government here, but their role in the family remained caught in the past.

Yet surprisingly the practice of homosexuality is accepted, even legal, in Costa Rica after a citizen has reached the age of consent—legally defined as 15 years old. There are laws, too, against homophobia and prohibiting discrimination on the basis of sexual orientation. Add to that enlightened legal stance the anything-goes attitude in the depths of San Jose, and Dean's choice of Costa Rica made a lot more sense.

Since San Jose was a transshipment point for cocaine and heroin from South America, Dean would have no trouble finding recreational drugs.

Dean adjusted rapidly to the no-holds-barred approach of the inner city, and participated in the exuberant and wild night life. At 11 P.M., discos were full, and with $200,000 in his pocket, Dean was ready to party hard. Nightly, he mingled with the crowds until the first rays of sun streaked across the tropical horizon.

CHAPTER TWENTY-FIVE

DR. LAURIE POLIS HEARD THROUGH THE GRAPEVINE THAT Dean had gotten out on bail and fled the country. She assumed that neither local authorities nor Interpol were interested in wasting the time and money to find him, or to extradite him, when all he faced was a possible sentence of 4 years. Dean Faiello, she thought, was no longer a threat—just a low-level fugitive of interest to no one. She did not hear his name again for many months.

IN OCTOBER, INVESTIGATOR DELLA ROCCA FINALLY GOT THE search warrant providing the authorization to access Maria's email account. In it, he discovered his first strong lead. Maria had an appointment with a Doctor Faiello on April 13. Dean appeared to be the last person to see Maria alive. Della Rocca wanted to talk to him. *But where was he?*

In no time, Della Rocca sniffed out Dean's recent legal troubles. That led him to Dean's attorney Margaret Shalley, but she had no idea of Dean's whereabouts.

THAT SAME MONTH, DEBRA FAIELLO RECEIVED AN EMAIL FROM Dean with instructions on what he needed done. She followed them to the letter. She ransomed Dean's Jeep Cherokee from the New Jersey impound lot. She and

Patty Rosado went to Mark Ritchey's house and retrieved the title to the car. Later, Debra transferred the vehicle to her name.

While at Mark's place, Debra and Patty picked up Dean's furniture and all of his patient files. They also took possession of the piece of luggage Mark had found—the one containing Maria Cruz's purse.

At this point, Greg Bach thought that Dean's worst deeds had been inflicted on him. He knew Dean skipped town leaving Mark Ritchey with a pile of bills, and owing money to Stephen Schwartz. But none of those debts approached the magnitude of what Greg was owed.

How does Dean get away with this crap? Greg wondered. *Because people let him.* And at that moment, Greg decided to stop being one of those people.

Through a friend, Greg learned that Dean had a new business partner—a man with a wife and children. He felt a moral obligation to find this person, wherever he was, and to warn him before he, too, was left penniless. Greg could not remain silent. *But where was Dean?*

AROUND THIS SAME TIME, GREG BACH LEARNED THAT THE ATtorney general's office was looking for Dean. He called Ronda Lustman, the prosecutor who had led the state's case against Dean for practicing medicine without a license, to find out if she knew Dean's whereabouts. She didn't have a clue.

"If you have any information about Dean's credit card accounts," Lustman suggested, "it would help us track him down." However, Greg no longer had access to any of that information.

He did have one tidbit for Lustman. He told her about the telephone call Martin Mannert, Dean's accountant, had received back in April, in which Dean mentioned a woman he rushed to the hospital.

Ronda wanted Greg to share this information with Brian Ford, the investigator in the attorney general's office covering the case. She thought it was something Brian would want to look into. At first, Greg was reluctant to make the call. Despite everything, he still cared for Dean. For two months, Greg tried to put it all out of his mind and get on with his life. But no matter how hard he tried, it haunted him.

Just before the holidays, Greg placed a call to Investigator Ford. Ford said that they just couldn't figure out why Dean would disappear. "He hasn't done anything that bad. Maybe it was because we wanted to question him about a missing person—a woman."

"What missing person?" Greg asked.

"Maria Cruz."

The name meant nothing to Greg. "Was she a client?"

"Yes."

Greg told Ford about his conversation with Martin Mannert. He said that Dean had called in a panic because one of his patients, who was seeing him for the removal of a tattoo, passed out after he administered a local anesthetic. The patient had recovered, Martin told Greg, after Dean rushed her to St. Vincent's hospital.

"I want to know more," Ford said. "We'll get on this right after the holidays. I'll call you back then."

Greg then called Martin, hoping to learn more about the patient who passed out. "He said she had no vital signs," Martin offered.

That's far worse than passing out, Greg thought. "Do you remember when this happened?" he asked.

All Martin could remember was that it was in the spring. Greg prodded Martin's memory, trying to stir up a connection to some other event or to a particular date. Finally, something jiggled loose. "I know it was about the same time that Dean locked you out of the house."

Greg pulled out his planner and narrowed down the date: April 13. *Did he* kill *her? If he did, where would he put the body?* The questions rolled through Greg's head for days, dark and grotesque scenarios playing out in his mind. He knew a large old home like Dean's in Newark had lots nooks and crannies for hiding objects large and small. He didn't known if Dean was capable of such a horrible act but the logic of the possibility made sense to him.

Mentally, Greg traveled through the house at 212 Elwood. He moved from room to room, remembering details, peering in closets and crannies, trying to determine where the best hiding place might be. *Where could he stash a body without the new owners finding it?*

His head full of visions of the house, Greg went to a home on Park Avenue to fulfill a contract to decorate a Christmas tree. In the middle of hanging ornaments, Greg's mind raced to the carriage house, the memory of Dean pouring concrete flashing before his eyes. Before he knew it, he had blurted the whole story out to the woman assisting him. She burst into tears.

Up until then, Greg thought he was being paranoid, allowing his imagination to run amok. Now, he believed his suspicions that Dean killed someone were true.

CHAPTER TWENTY-SIX

AS A COSMOPOLITAN CENTER IN CENTRAL AMERICA, SAN JOSE was a relative newcomer. It did not develop into a city of any size until the late 1800s. As a result, it does not have the strong colonial flavor often associated with cities in that region. Although there are some graceful old buildings in the heart of town, the structures that dominate San Jose's landscape were erected during the building boom of the 1950s and -60s.

The streets of San Jose sprawl across the city in a manner similar to those of Manhattan. Numbered *calles*—streets—stretch in one direction intersecting numbered *avenidas*—avenues—running perpendicular. Unlike Manhattan, though, even-numbered streets and avenues are stacked on one side of the city center—odd-numbered ones on the other.

On the surface, the consistency of this pattern would suggest an easy set-up to learn and navigate, but there is one sticking point. No businesses or residences have street addresses in all of Costa Rica. *Josefinos* use intersections and landmarks to give directions.

Unfortunately for newcomers like Dean, in San Jose, as in any vital urban center, change is constant. Yesterday's landmark gives way to today's parking lot. However, locals seldom provide such significant details. For example, the Coca-Cola building is mentioned with great frequency, even though it's been a bus depot for years.

Dean's ability to find his way around the city was hampered by that eccentricity, as well as the language barrier. English-only North Americans flock to a neighborhood called Gringo Gulch and mingle with bilingual ex-pats. They congregate in its hotels, its McDonald's and at its many bars, including the New York Bar and Nashville South.

There, imported drinks come with a very high price tag. *Ticos* rely on *guaro*, a harsh spirit distilled from fermented sugar cane, local beers, like Bavaria and Imperial, and a selection of wines. Unlike the vintages made up North, these wines are not made from grapes, but from spiny palm sap or from blackberries and other locally grown fruits.

In the evening, a plethora of discothèques and dance halls fling open their doors and blast music into the streets. Entry is free or cheap. With drinks, they serve *bocas*, heaping plates of appetizers like *cerviche*, chicken wings and bean soup. No matter the musical taste—or the sexual preference—there is a club for everyone.

Dean soon found his favorite spots to frolic in the gay night life of San Jose. He spent many nights at El CantaBrico at Calle 11 and Avenida 3, where the focus was on drinking and meeting men.

Another of Dean's favored hang-outs, Pucho's Night Club, had a regular set of drag queens and male strip-tease acts. A block and a half away was Bochinche, a velvet-roped, multi-leveled disco with huge video screens, and drag queen routines that alternated with DJ's playing dance music.

Businesses that catered to gay clientele extended beyond nightclubs. There were bathhouses like Jano and Paris. Hispalis, an upscale sauna—the largest in Central

America—boasted twenty-five years of experience providing treatment and service for men.

There was even a gay-friendly Internet café, 1@10, near the Plaza de la Cultura in the center of town. They lured gay patrons with a $1-an-hour access rate and a promise that 1@10 was "the place to go where you can be yourself." Typically, though, Dean checked his email—two or three times a week—at the Cyber Café on Avenida 2.

From there, he sent emails to friends in New York. To one, Dean claimed he had left town because of a botched tattoo removal, in which the patient had to be hospitalized. Of course, he never mentioned the real secret, left buried in Newark.

DEAN HAD A COURT DATE IN MANHATTAN ON OCTOBER 8, 2003. He did not make it. His attorney, Margaret Shalley, admitted to the judge that she had no idea of her client's current whereabouts. The court ruled that Dean's bail was forfeit. Dean Faiello was now officially a fugitive from justice. A new date for sentencing was set for December. That day came and went, and still no sign of Dean. The judge issued a warrant for his arrest.

When a bail bondsman sent Greg a bill for $6,000, he was confused. The original bail amount was $5,000 and he'd already given the company $2,500. Why was the bill higher than the balance on the bond? Before he could figure out the situation, the bond company went out of business. That debt, at least, was off Greg's back.

SAN JOSE KICKED OFF THE 2003 HOLIDAY SEASON WITH THE *Festival de la Luz*—Festival of Lights. More than a million people gathered for the night-time parade with its light-adorned floats and elaborate fireworks display. Dean loved the color and celebration of Christmas and threw himself into the unique elements of the festivities in a foreign land.

The *ticos'* spirit of celebration is enhanced by the *aguinaldo*, a government-mandated Christmas bonus each worker receives from his employer—the equivalent of one month's pay. Costa Rica pioneered this concept in Latin America, and their example of Christmas largesse is now mimicked by other countries in the hemisphere.

Homes bustled with holiday activity as families prepared their personal *portal*, a nativity scene that was often an ambitious life-sized project taking up an entire room. Bright tropical flowers and colorful fresh fruit decorated the displays.

Dean was amused to see the Christmas tree he knew in the States replaced here with a new tradition: a big evergreen branch, a small cypress tree or several dried coffee branches decorated with white paint, brilliant strips of paper, colored balls, small figurines and lace, and topped with a gold star to represent the Star of Bethlehem. As he walked through the city, he saw door after door of homes and businesses decorated with cypress wreaths trimmed with red coffee beans and ribbons, and strings of multicolored lights that made the city glow. Everywhere, he heard heart-felt greeting of *Feliz Navidad*. He walked through the *Zapote* section of San Jose watching it come to life with an improvised amusement park filled with rides, games of chance and food booths.

On Christmas Eve, the celebration became more insular, and Dean was an outsider as families gathered at their churches for *Misa de Gallo*, a special holiday service, afterwards enjoying the traditional Christmas dinner featuring chicken and pork tamales stuffed with potatoes and vegetables and wrapped in plantain leaves. The adults wash their meal down with rum punch or *rompope*—eggnog laced with dark rum or brandy. For the children, they serve *aguadulce*, a sweet, fruit-based beverage. A quiet descended over the night club scene as doors shut so that employees could join their families.

It all cut loose again the day after Christmas with Dean parading in the thick of the *tope*. Originally a prelude to a bull fight, consisting of men on horseback, the procession Dean saw had developed into much more. In addition to equestrian performances, *caballo*-drawn carriages and oxcarts trailed through the street. Floats, marching bands, dancing girls and clowns added to the festive atmosphere. As it wended its way through the byways of San Jose, revelers mingled and celebrated. The party did not stop until January 6, the day traditionally observed for the arrival of the Magi.

It was an intoxicating season in San Jose—a month-long celebration of drink and good cheer. And in 2003, Dean partied through the whole holiday—all day and all night long.

For the Cruz family, on the other hand, that Christmas was a solemn occasion: Maria was still missing. Nine months had come and gone and still no sign of her. The traditional high spirits of the Filipino Christmas—one that rivaled Costa Rica's for its length and exuberance—were muted. The Cruzes went through the motions, but any feelings of renewal or good cheer were lost under the shadow of the mystery of Maria. The pain went even deeper in her parents' hearts, her disappearance coming as it did before the first time in more than a decade that Maria planned to return to the Philippines for Christmas. *Where was she?*

CHAPTER TWENTY-SEVEN

GREG WAITED TO HEAR BACK FROM BRIAN FORD. THE HOLI-days came and went. Still, the investigator did not call. Greg grew annoyed, not realizing until much later that Ford was doing all he could to convince others to pursue Greg's lead. Once there was a possible homicide, however, it was no longer Ford's case. The investigative responsibility moved from the attorney general's office to the detective bureau of the New York Police Department.

Greg sat down and composed a letter to Ford, describing the haunting scenario that played on a continuous loop in his mind. He wrote of Dean pouring a concrete slab and added his suspicion that it wasn't big enough to conceal a whole human body. In closing, he asked that, whether he was right or wrong, he really would like to hear back from Ford.

Greg went to the mailbox, envelope in hand. Suddenly, having it all down in writing intimidated him. It was so final. He stood rooted to the sidewalk, the letter burning in his hand. He knew it was a betrayal of the man he loved. He knew that if he mailed it, there was no turning back—ever. Greg didn't want to hurt Dean—but he did want to do the right thing.

He pulled down the metal door and slid the letter inside. It hit the pile of mail in the bottom of the box with a muted thump. For a few moments, Greg could not move. He had the sensation of having just stepped off of a steep cliff.

He waited for a response with a numb mind. He paid close attention to the local news, suspecting that if he was right, he'd hear word there that someone had taken action. Although it was unlikely, he continued to hope that somehow the authorities would disprove his suspicions. He hung in limbo not knowing what, if anything, he should do.

Greg didn't hear from Ford or any other official for weeks, but he did connect with a friend—one who'd recently gotten a lengthy email from Dean. In it, Dean described his tropical home, complaining that no one in Costa Rica spoke English. The friend was concerned that she'd get in trouble for communicating with a fugitive.

Greg didn't think getting an email was a crime, but he encouraged her paranoia just the same. Contact the authorities, he urged her. Maybe if they wouldn't respond to him, they would respond to someone else. "If you talk to them," he told her, "please tell them to call me."

She did talk to police, who came to her house and picked up a hard copy of the email that same day. The next day, Joe Della Rocca visited Greg. When Greg told him about the concrete slab and his concern that a part of a body or other evidence could be hidden within, Della Rocca said, "Faiello's too smart to do something like that."

"Is it smart to get busted for practicing medicine and then start practicing medicine again? Is that very smart?" Greg retorted.

"You've got a point," Della Rocca said.

CHAPTER TWENTY-EIGHT

THE ISSUE SURROUNDING JASON OPSAHL'S PENSION WAS AT last resolved after the first of the new year—in Dean's favor. Debra and Patty visited attorney Tom Shanahan and pressured him to give them Dean's money. They said that was what Dean wanted. Shanahan balked—Debra was not his client, Dean was. He asked Debra where Dean was, and she responded, "You don't want to know."

The duo returned again, leaning on Shanahan to wire the money to a bank in Costa Rica. Neither Debra nor Patty mentioned that Dean was a fugitive on charges of practicing medicine without a license. Tom insisted on speaking with Dean before he did anything with the money.

Dean called Shanahan and explained, "I'm taking a long vacation from my troubles with my business partners. I'm in the jungle."

At his request, in early February, Shanahan wired $50,000 to Banco Popular in San Jose to the account of Dean Faiello. With this inheritance in hand, Dean began squandering extravagant sums of money as he explored more of the country.

Debra Faiello, on the other hand, assuaged her guilt with a concession to Jason's memory. She made a contribution of $5,000 to Broadway Cares/Equity Fights AIDS.

Dean left San Jose by way of the country's roller-coaster

roads. He traversed miles of bumpy terrain before reaching the main highway, where vendors hawking sunglasses, cell phone accessories and baseball caps lined the sides of the road.

He left the ring of mountains surrounding the Central Valley on the Pan-American Highway, the same road that connects Tierra del Fuego at the southernmost point of the Americas to Alaska at the north. He passed through a mosaic of forest, pasture, and farmland.

Leaving the Pan-American highway, Dean caught the route built in the 1800s to transport coffee beans by ox-carts from farms to the ports on the coast—and from there to the cities of Europe.

He entered an active geological fault zone with deep depressions in the road bed, approaching and then crossing over the crest. The highway then descended toward the coastline of the Gulf of Nicoya.

A couple hours after leaving San Jose, Dean had entered Esparza—one of the oldest towns in Costa Rica, just twenty kilometers inland from Puntarenas. It was a sleepy little village with clean streets and laid-back townfolk. The quaint village square was lined with cobblestones and featured an octagonal gazebo and a bust of the founder of Esparza, Diego de Artieda y Cherino—a Spanish Governor of Costa Rica.

He rented a home there under the name Diego Faiello. After spending a few days relaxing in an atmosphere far removed from the crowded streets of San Jose, Dean moved on, farther north to the Pacific Coast and the Villas Playa Samara, a beachfront hotel with spacious Mediterranean-style villas where the heady scent of tropical blooms blended with the tang of the ocean air to create a fragrance like none other. The lush, manicured grounds echoed with the brazen squawks of exotic birds and the mournful cries of howler monkeys.

Dean requested the best accommodations possible when he checked in, paying cash in advance for three nights. At the doorstep of his three-bedroom villa, a seven-kilometer stretch of virginal white sand beach lay at his feet, with ground-hugging vines of beach beans and matapalo. Unlike much of Costa Rica's Pacific Coast, where wild waves pound the shore, this spot was not a haven for surfers. A long coral reef protected this stretch of waterfront, making the waves kiss the sand with a gentleness that felt as timid as an apology.

Villas Playa Samara was heaven for nature lovers. Iguanas struck noble poses in the sun. Dolphins arced into the air on the horizon. Endangered giant sea turtles laid eggs on a nearby patch of beach, and scenic boat trips on the nearby Tempisque River offered an adventure in wonder. Every evening, the sun descended into the Pacific Ocean in a breathtaking medley of color.

Dean, however, spent the greater part of his days sunning by the pool and getting refills at the swim-up poolside bar. He downed Coronas, piña coladas, Cuba Libres and double vodkas with melon juice, running up a daily bar bill of $200 or more.

He found Leo the bartender very attractive, and night after night invited him back to his room. However, Dean's charming, seductive ways did not win over Leo.

"Where are you from?" Leo asked.

"New York."

"What is your profession?"

"Well, I am a doctor."

"Really?"

"I am a man of mystery. I have a lot of problems. Don't ask me too many questions."

CHAPTER TWENTY-NINE

DEAN MAY HAVE BEEN ABLE TO SUPPRESS THE CURIOSITY OF a staff devoted to pleasing him, but he couldn't stop the queries that Detective Della Rocca was making miles away back in Manhattan. Greg Bach's story from the previous May gave birth to a lot of questions in Della Rocca's mind.

Two case files—one for a fugitive from justice that had sent Investigator Ford looking for a phony doctor, and the other for a missing persons complaint about the baffling disappearance of a young woman—were now blending into one. As they pushed their puzzle together, the two detectives found that all the pieces seemed to fit.

On February 13, 2004, Detective Della Rocca drove out to Newark and spoke with Jeffrey Ransom and a woman named Loretta who both lived at 212 Elwood. He asked if he could take a look inside the adjacent carriage house at 214 Elwood. They gave their consent.

His visual inspection confirmed Greg Bach's story of a hand-troweled concrete slab of recent vintage. He looked around but saw no blood. He stood still and sniffed the air—a little mustiness, but no whiff of decay. And that would make sense. It had been nine months since the body was sealed up in its concrete tomb. Della Rocca looked at the rough-poured slab in the back and suddenly knew Greg's suspicions were true. *So far, so good*, he thought. *Maybe the long wait for the Cruz family is finally over.*

But in Newark, Della Rocca was out of his jurisdiction—in another state under a different legal authority. So he enlisted the assistance of the homicide squad in the Essex County Prosecutor's Office. Investigator Christopher Smith and Assistant Prosecutor Thomas McTigue walked Della Rocca through the unfamiliar paperwork needed to obtain a search warrant for the carriage house.

New Jersey Superior Court Judge Michael Petrolle authorized the search. New York authorities could not go in alone. On February 18, investigators Della Rocca, Smith and Ford, and Della Rocca's partner T. J. Marony came to the scene with the Newark Police Department. The police called in for the assistance of the New Jersey troopers. En masse, a team of forensic technicians and detectives descended on the unsuspecting neighborhood of Forest Hill to tear apart the concrete and gather evidence in the case of Maria Cruz.

It was impossible for this many people and vehicles to go unnoticed. Just two and a half years after 9-11, in a community not far from the collapse of the twin towers, it was not surprising that the most popular rumor involved Islamic extremists. Word spread that the authorities were busting a terrorist cell. The first news helicopter headed to Newark and in no time, every media outlet with an air crew was there. Even the Department of Homeland Security and the FBI sent agents to the scene.

At the center of the circus, techs got to work dismantling the concrete mound by the carriage house steps. The digging began at noon. Concerned about the destruction of Jeffrey's property, Loretta questioned the police officers.

"We'll dig up the whole floor of the garage if we need

to," they told her. "If we find nothing there, we'll dig up your whole yard." Then they threatened her with arrest if she interfered in any way.

As Loretta left the carriage house, she heard one officer mention Greg Bach's name. She headed for the telephone. She didn't have his phone number, but she knew who Greg was. She wanted to talk to him and find out what the heck was happening.

Two hours later, techs removed a suitcase from Dean's concrete creation. News photographers snapped photos as officers carried two bundles from the building to the awaiting vans. Officials continued to search for evidence implicating Dean Faiello in the death of Maria Cruz.

Maria's Uncle Jose in Queens held out hope. He told *The New York Times*: "Everyone is so very sure that it's Maria. I'm still clinging to the hope that it's not really her. They'll be doing the autopsy tomorrow morning."

Nonetheless, Irenea and Rudolfo Cruz, along with their two oldest children Tes and Jun, boarded a plane in Manila for their sorrowful flight to Newark Liberty International Airport. With confirmation of Maria's death, there would come the demise of all their hopes and all their dreams.

DR. DAVID GOLDSCHMITT, EMERGENCY SERVICES DIRECTOR AT New York University Downtown Hospital, backed out of his driveway to head to work. Looking up Ridge Street, he saw the yellow crime-scene tape circling a major portion of the block. His first thoughts went to a friend of his whose home was enclosed inside the police barrier. As soon as he arrived at the hospital, he sent an email to her. "Are you okay?" he asked.

The response contained a grisly truth, one that churned

in his stomach and made bile rise in his throat. The telephone conversation he'd had with Dean ten months ago raced through his mind.

Did he overhear a murder? *It couldn't be connected,* he thought, then called one of his neighbors. As he listened to a story about the body recently removed, he encouraged himself not to think the worst. *Maybe I'm just being paranoid*, his cautious side argued. But David's sense of responsibility and respect for life—any life—drove him to the Newark police station after work to tell them what he knew.

JEANE MACINTOSH HAD TRAVELED OUT TO NEW JERSEY THAT morning to cover another story. Finishing her assignment, she turned back to Manhattan. As she approached Newark, Jeane noticed the flash of helicopters flitting through the sky. Curiosity danced in her mind, but she continued on toward the office.

Before she hit the river to cross over to New York, her cell phone rang. It was the assignment desk. "Jeane, does the name Dean Faiello mean anything to you?"

"Yeah," Jean said, "that's my fake doctor."

"They're looking for a body at his house in Newark. They think he murdered Maria Cruz."

Jeane turned her car around and headed back toward the hovering helicopters.

LETICIA FRANKS, DEAN'S NEIGHBOR ON RIDGE STREET, returned from a shopping trip to discover her whole block closed off by strips of yellow crime-scene tape. There were more police vehicles gathered in her block than she'd ever seen in one place at one time.

She had to park a distance from her home and walk, lugging her packages to the house. From her porch, she saw the bustle of activity in the carriage house that faced Ridge Street. She didn't know her new neighbor Jeffrey Ransom that well and wondered what he had done.

Then she learned that her new neighbor wasn't the problem at all. It was the polite young man who passed the time with her, helped her out with her porch and tantalized the neighborhood girls—he was responsible for the police and media attention. Even worse—a body had been found only yards from her front door. She sat in silent disbelief, rebuffing every media representative who darkened her door.

LINDA BURKE HEARD THE NEWS OF THE GROTESQUE DISCOVERY in New Jersey. Then she heard the suspect's name—Dean Faiello. *Why did that name sound so familiar?*

For days, the question lingered in the back of her mind until her memory sparked. *Wasn't that the name of the dermatologist who treated me when I first moved to New York seven years ago?*

The revelation sent her scurrying to her financial records. She dug deep and there it was—the receipt for services rendered. She was right: It was Dean Faiello. She had lain down on a table and placed herself at the mercy of someone capable of burying a patient in concrete. She was horrified.

BARBARA NEVINS TAYLOR WAS SHOCKED WHEN SHE HEARD THE news. She had seen Faiello arrested and taken away in handcuffs. His arrest was supposed to end the charade—to stop him from performing risky procedures and posing as a doctor. And if he didn't do so on his own, she was confident that the cops would act to protect the public.

"You think if you expose a problem and show a bad guy doing something wrong, those in authority will prevent him from harming others," she said. "I can't believe they didn't keep an eye on him. He had a prior record—his past behavior foreshadowed his future actions. They should have known that."

When Channel 9 announced the discovery of Maria's body, they reprised their previous investigation of 2002. It was an indictment of the inefficiency of a vast, unwieldy bureaucracy. Barbara believed that if the authorities had acted more expeditiously, Maria Cruz would still be alive.

DANI SAMUELSON, A FORMER TRANSEXUAL CLIENT OF DEAN'S, watched NY1, the 24-hour local news channel, on February 18. Three times an hour, reporters recapped the news from Newark. When the story was repeated several times without any new information, Dani walked away, leaving the television on.

She sat at her computer tapping away, the news a constant, quiet hum in the background. Then she heard the announcer say, "Dean Faiello." Or at least that's what it sounded like. Dani's fingers froze over the keyboard. Was she imagining things? She rushed back to the television and turned up the volume, waiting for the news from Newark to cycle through again.

She was right. The announcer did say "Dean Faiello." He buried a woman's body in concrete at his house in Newark. Charming, gracious, good-looking Dean Faiello a killer? Unbelievable. Or was it?

Did the sinister truth always lurk beneath that attractive façade? The more she thought about it, the more believable it became. She recalled Howard Stern's reaction to the 1993 World Trade Center bombing. After the incident, every time Stern said an Arab name, he'd say "Guilty."

Dani now felt the same way about Dean. Whenever she heard his name, "Guilty" pounded through her head. Sometimes, she said it out loud.

CHAPTER THIRTY

DR. LAURIE POLIS WAS STAGGERED BY THE DISCOVERY OF A body at Dean Faiello's former home. She could barely set down the receiver before the phone rang again. Every member of the media she'd ever heard of—and a few she hadn't—called, wanting to know the back story of Dean Faiello.

Reporters cajoled her for interviews. They said: "You're the good guy," "You're the poster child for public protection," "You're the one who fought so hard to get him off the street." No amount of flattery swayed Dr. Polis. She would not agree to an interview. She did not want to win publicity out of Maria's victimization and Dean Faiello's handiwork.

GREG BACH WAS WORKING OUT AT THE GYM WHEN HIS CELL phone chirped. It was one of his old neighbors from Newark. Loretta called him, he told Greg. The police were tearing up the concrete in the carriage house and Loretta heard an officer mention Greg's name. "Could you call her and let her know what's going on?"

Greg could hardly believe it. At long last, the police acted on his information—state troopers and other officials filled that corner of the neighborhood to everyone's amazement. Soon Greg learned that not only had they acted, they also confirmed his worst suspicions. There was a body buried in the concrete he had watched Dean pour that ugly day in May.

Greg's thoughts went to the elderly housekeeper Elizabeth. While Dean's real estate broker was trying to sell his house, she met Elizabeth. Both spoke Hungarian and the two hit it off right away. They chattered in Elizabeth's native tongue every time the agent came to the house.

After negotiating a sale for Dean, the broker got a good price for Elizabeth's own home, enabling her to move from Newark to Ohio to be near her son. Elizabeth—now pushing 80—was scheduled to move early that morning. Greg hoped she left before the word about Dean spread to her door. He hoped she would never learn about what Dean had done. Greg knew it would break her heart.

By the time Greg returned to his apartment, messages from the media saturated his voicemail. He stopped answering the phone.

He was astonished that the police had leaked his name, that his involvement in the discovery of the body was revealed to the news outlets. Greg willingly told his story to authorities, but did not want Dean to know of his actions. From his viewpoint, the revelation of his name demonstrated a total disregard for his privacy and personal safety. Would Dean—could Dean—retaliate?

Watching the news the day that Maria was found, he heard that the body was hidden inside a suitcase. When Della Rocca and Marony visited him at his apartment that night, he asked, "Was she found in a suitcase?" but Della Rocca denied it.

When Greg later heard a full description of the black carry-on with wheels, he wondered why the cops would lie. He could recall that suitcase very well: It had been in the garage. Then, he'd noticed, it was gone. At one point, it returned. The suitcase was an odd presence, but with all the moving around of household items at the time, he did not give it much thought. After all, it sure did not seem big enough to hold a human body. But still, he thought, if the officers had told him the truth, his recollections might have been useful in their investigation. Greg simply did not understand their motivation.

He also did not comprehend their process of investigation. "You need to locate Dean's Jeep Cherokee," he told them. "Someone I know received an email from Dean. He'd inadvertently attached a document to it that provided instructions about locating and retrieving the vehicle. I think you'll find a New Jersey State Trooper with the car in her driveway." Greg said, alluding to Debra. "I think Dean used it to transport the body. It could contain forensic evidence."

"Ah, well," Della Rocca said in his heavy New York accent. "It's probably been all cleaned up by now."

Greg recoiled at that cavalier attitude. "While you're turning over every stone, why don'tcha just take a look at that one?"

The detective only shrugged in response. Nothing was making any sense to Greg at all.

AT FIRST, AUTHORITIES ANNOUNCED A TENTATIVE, PRELIMInary identification. From the serial number on the breast implants, it appeared as if the body was indeed Maria Cruz, who had been missing since April of the previous year. During autopsy, a forensic odontologist compared Maria's dental records with the mouth of the victim uncovered in Newark. There was a match. Maria Cruz had been found.

THE POLICE DISAPPEARED FROM THE NEIGHBORHOOD AFTER A couple of days; but for weeks afterward, bedlam reigned in Forest Hill—what had been the last quiet neighborhood in Newark. Local television vans, newspaper reporters and stringers for national news services formed an occupation force in the vicinity of Elwood and Ridge.

Maria Cruz's family made pilgrimages to the spot. They parked their car across the street and stared at the old white carriage house where their daughter had lain encased in cold concrete for month after month. Neighbors watched them, but left them in peace—their hearts broken in vicarious grief.

Maria's sister Tes told reporters, "You can't just allow somebody to die, and then throw her out like a piece of garbage. She must have had a family. Did he not think of that family?"

In their unquenchable thirst for a new angle, the media horde spread out from the immediate area. They formed outposts at every location with any connection—no matter how tenuous—to the crime. One spot was the emergency room at NYU's Downtown Hospital. Their presence interfered with the timely administration of critical care treatment. Officials told Dr. Goldschmitt to stay away from the facility until the furor died down.

When the media got word that Dean fled the area and was now in Central America, the satellite uplink trucks, microphones and questions diminished, but did not fade away for weeks. Some of the reporters grabbed at the opportunity to leave the New York winter behind and take up the hunt for a story on the sunny shores of Costa Rica.

DEBRA FAIELLO WAS NOT TO BLAME FOR MARIA CRUZ'S DEATH, but guilt dogged her steps just the same. She did have some knowledge of Dean's actions. Did she know about the murder when she assumed control of the vehicle used to transport Maria's body? Did she realize what Dean had done when she'd laid claim to Dean's patient files? Had she learned the identity of his victim when she gained possession of Maria's purse and identification? Was she part of the cover-up?

Only Debra knew the answers to those questions. It was clear however that she knew her brother had broken the law by providing treatments that he wasn't qualified to give. She knew he forged prescriptions to feed his drug habit.

Debra, a member of law enforcement, knew her brother was on the lam. She knew his whereabouts when she badgered Tom Shanahan to send him that money. She duped an upstanding and respected member of the legal community by withholding information. By doing so, had she implicated herself in a conspiracy to aid and abet a fugitive from justice?

The moment Tom Shanahan heard about the body found at Dean's home, he called the district attorney's office and informed them that he had unwittingly wired funds to the account of a wanted fugitive in Costa Rica. He said nothing more about Dean. No matter what Dean had done, he was still Tom's client, and attorney–client privilege prevailed.

Shanahan felt he could ethically reveal Debra's involvement in Dean's flight if he received a criminal subpoena from the New Jersey State Police. Brad Hamilton, a *New York Post* reporter, agreed to attempt to broker that deal.

He called the Internal Affairs division and explained the situation. "This person wants to speak with you," he said, "but can't do so unless you issue a subpoena."

"We don't work that way. We don't issue subpoenas to get information," the sergeant said.

"But he wants to talk to you," Brad said.

"Then, let him talk."

Brad wondered what lay behind the answers. *Were the New Jersey State police willing to ignore the possibility of wrongdoing by one of their own?*

CHAPTER THIRTY-ONE

ON SUNDAY, FEBRUARY 22, FRIENDS, RELATIVES—INCLUDING Maria's parents and siblings from the Philippines—and co-workers from Barclays gathered at the Greenwich Village Funeral Home on Bleecker Street for a two-hour prayer service in memory of Maria Cruz. The Bukas Palad Choir from Irvington, New Jersey, sang *"Hindi Kita Malilimutan."* This sorrowful melody in Maria's native Tagalog dialect meant "We Will Never Forget You."

The funeral mass began at 9:30 on the morning of February 23 at Our Lady of Pompeii Church on the corner of Carmine and Bleecker Streets in Greenwich Village. A dominant landmark in this area of Manhattan, the Italian Renaissance–style church, with its asymmetrically placed tower, was built in 1928 on property that once was the site of a vaudeville hall and also of St. Benedict Moor, the first black Catholic church in New York City.

Constructed to serve the Italian-Americans who established the surrounding neighborhood, the church continued to offer one mass in Italian every Sunday. The congregation, however, was now far more diverse. In response to an influx of immigrants from the Philippines, the church established their Filipino Pastoral Ministry in the 1980s. Many Vietnamese worshiped regularly at Our

Lady of Pompeii and a mass in Portuguese often brought a full house of Brazilians through its doors.

On the day of Maria's funeral, more than seventy people filled the pews of the sanctuary, surrounded by marble columns, frescoes and murals. Rudolfo Cruz clutched the back of the pew before him—the pressure of his grief-strengthened grip turning his fingertips white.

Reverend Erno Diaz officiated over the service. He spoke of Maria's becoming, in her short life, the embodiment of the American dream. "She came from the Philippines to make it in New York. And, of course, with her brains, with her determination, and also with her courage—she made it."

Maria's older sister, Tes, delivered the eulogy, first addressing her words to her sister: "You were a very big dreamer. You were not afraid to move out of your comfort zone—away from your family, away from the life you had always known—to face challenges, hurdle obstacles, do whatever it takes to make your dreams come true.

"I guess, because honesty was second nature to you, you expected the same from others. But, my dear sister, I think you expected too much, because not everybody you trusted were trustworthy after all."

To the gathered mourners, Tes said, "Pipay was a very special person. She left a legacy that nothing in this world is more important than to treasure one's family."

As the casket was carried out of the church, Rudolfo wailed, and his son, Jun, rested his hands on his father's shoulders—in shared grief and in the hope of granting comfort. Rebecca de los Angeles, Maria's aunt, embraced her sister Irenea, as she sobbed out her sorrow over the loss of her daughter.

Maria's body slid into the hearse. Family members patted the wood of her coffin, shouting, "I love you. I love you."

"It's the saddest moment of my life," Rudolfo said.

After the service, Maria's body was cremated—her remains hermetically sealed in a heavy bronze urn. Her family flew her ashes back to the Philippines on Saturday, February 28.

Days of continuous wake followed her arrival in her native land. Hundreds of Maria's relatives and friends attended, offering words of consolation and hugs of empathy. Then, Maria was laid to rest in a serene mausoleum with white granite floors at the Manila Memorial Park in Paranaque City on the outskirts of Manila.

Her parents visited her every day.

CHAPTER THIRTY-TWO

AS WITH OTHER TRAGIC DEATHS IN THE INTERNET AGE, CHAT rooms exploded with messages from anyone with even marginal awareness of Dean Faiello or Maria Cruz. A resident of Forest Hill wrote:

> My partner who is a glutton for gossip is following this story avidly. We live about two blocks from the compound where Maria Jeritza lived. The lady that cleaned house for us up until August of last year also cleaned the guest house that Dean Faiello, the fake plastic surgeon lived in. She has since moved to Ohio but I wonder if she knows anything. She was always telling stories.

Another voice chimed in,

> Hey, that guy goes to my gym. His locker was a few over from mine. Haven't seen him for several months. Now I know why. Black boxer briefs, by the way.

Some Internet users came to Dean's defense:

> Dean was not a scheming plotting murderer; however the path that he took was very much crooked. If anyone

saw the movie *Sunset Boulevard*, Dean could have played the part of Gloria Swanson to a tee. His crumbling Elwood Avenue home was a reflection of his personal/social aspirations. Unfortunately, Dean's use of drugs, alcohol and his greed have extinguished the wonderful life of Maria Cruz and the energy invested by her loving family.

Another made this comment:

Dean's life went out of control, but he is no sadistic murderer. The fact that he called people to try to save her indicates that he panicked when things started to go awry. The man would not kill a bug, let alone a human, on purpose. He told someone the only time he was happy was when he was taking drugs. What a sad commentary on what could have been a beautiful life. Where will it go from here? I and many others hope his punishment leaves him enough time to make something of his life.

In response to these compassionate opinions, another writer expressed outrage.

Are you people crazy? Dean killed someone, was practicing illegally and then tried to cover up this poor girl's death! I have no empathy for him or anyone else like him. To top off everything he's done, he fled the country in hopes of not having to take responsibility for his actions! Get a grip!

Others on line remembered Maria.

I'm stepping back into the blogosphere for a quick break and am greeted with sad news. The remains of

Maria Cruz who went missing last April seem to have been found. Maria Cruz was friends with women I worked with at my old job, and her poster was all over Midtown Manhattan last spring. I hope that knowing what happened to her, though the answer to the questions is tragic, is some comfort to them.

Another posted:

I met Maria while I was working at Barclay's on a contract. I just remember her as cute and smiling a lot. I wanted to ask her out someday but never did. She was always nice to people. I saw her uncle putting up posters in my neighborhood and I immediately recognized her—it was the first time I made the choice to pray for someone's safety who wasn't a family member. I just remember this sweet girl who wouldn't hurt a fly.

JEANE MACINTOSH OF THE *NEW YORK POST* GOT A TIP THAT Dean Faiello had sent emails to friends from Costa Rica. She called the attorney general's office, but officials would not confirm Dean's presence there—nor would they deny it. And that was good enough for her.

Since she spoke no Spanish, Jeane grabbed Bolivar Arellano, a photographer with a high degree of fluency in the language, and wasted no time in getting to Costa Rica. She arrived on February 20, just two days after the discovery of Maria's body. Jeane was the first U.S. journalist investigating the case to touch down in San Jose.

Her first stop was the United States Embassy. "We haven't started looking for Dean Faiello," they said. "We don't have a warrant yet."

"We have pictures of him," Jeane said, flashing an array of shots of Dean from her coverage of his illegal practice of medicine charge back in 2002. "The D.A. told us they are going to issue a warrant."

"You have pictures?"

Jeane nodded. They asked her to keep in touch.

Next Jean and Bolivar paid a visit to Marco Badilla, head of immigration for Costa Rica. "We can't start looking for him until your government asks us to," he said. "We are eager to help, but we don't even have the basic information."

Jeane provided Marco with copies of her pictures of Dean in exchange for a copy of Dean's passport and his entry documents. Then the intrepid duo attempted to set up a meeting with Interpol. They were given directions to a nighttime rendezvous point, a dark spot by the railroad tracks lit only by the glimmer of a nearby McDonald's. Again they were told, "We can't look until we're asked."

Jeane and Bolivar hit the banks in San Jose, chasing down a rumor that Dean had recently received funds from the States via electronic transfer. At Banco Popular, tellers recognized Dean's photo right away. They directed Jeane to an Internet café in the town square.

"Yes," the woman at the café said in Spanish as Bolivar translated for Jeane. "He is here two, three times a week. He usually sits in this chair," she said placing her hand on the back of a seat in front of a computer. "You can wait for him here."

Jeane and Bolivar staked out the Internet café by day and prowled the clubs in the gay section of San Jose each night. At Pucho's, a woman recognized his picture and said, "I hired him as a go-go dancer."

"A go-go dancer?" Jeane asked, poking her finger at Dean's picture. "Are you sure? This guy's forty years old."

"Yes. He danced here for about a week. But I haven't seen him in weeks."

Jeane ran with the go-go dancer story. Local Costa Rican reporters followed up with the club's owner. He denied that Dean ever worked at Pucho's. He swore no one there had ever seen Dean. He was going to sue the *New York Post*, he said.

Jeane got a tip from Costa Rican authorities that Dean had moved to the coast. She put a plane and pilot on stand-by in case she and Bolivar needed to make a spur-of-the-moment flight west.

Following up on the tip, Jeane called Marco Badilla, who confirmed the story, but did not have a precise location. "We are expecting a warrant any time now," he said.

She called the district attorney's office in Manhattan, telling them what she knew and what she planned to do. "But we don't want to impede an investigation. What do you want us to do?"

They asked her to sit tight, saying that Dean would be arrested the next day. Jeane didn't have much choice. No one was telling her where along the 630 miles of Pacific coast Dean was staying—in fact, no one seemed to know with any certainty. One story placed him near the water, living with a woman in a house in a small village. Other tales placed him at an assortment of coastal resorts.

NEW YORK LAW ENFORCEMENT MADE PLANS TO SEND INVESTI-gators down to Costa Rica. Paperwork and formality slowed their progress. Prosecutors could not issue an arrest warrant for the murder of Maria Cruz until the medical examiner provided an autopsy report with his determination of the cause and manner of death. They could, though, issue a warrant for bail-jumping—and they did. That charge did not possess sufficient weight to make Dean eligible for extradition, but they thought it would be enough to place him behind bars in Costa Rica until additional charges could be filed.

While waiting for the prosecutor's office to take action, Detective Joe Della Rocca searched the apartment at 151 West 16th Street, where Maria lost her life. He found a laser machine, a box of syringes and an assortment of medications.

Investigators Brian Ford and Joe Buffolino of the state attorney general's office boarded a plane bound for Costa Rica on February 25—one week after Maria's body was found. That evening, Jeane and Bolivar entered the lobby of the Holiday Inn on their way out of the hotel. They saw Ford and Buffolino checking in. *Something's coming down soon*, Jeane thought.

The reporter and photographer headed out to the airport the next morning to confirm with their pilot that a flight was imminent. As they arrived, they saw Detectives Joe Della Rocca and Bob Jennings of the New York Police Department disembarking from a plane. Following them were a gaggle of reporters from New York.

After meeting with the pilot, Jeane and Bolivar headed straight back to their hotel. They discovered that nearly everyone they saw at the airport was now checking in to the Holiday Inn. With the arrival of the investigators from New York, the once-cooperative Costa Rican authorities clammed up. Her local sources went as dry as a desert.

The authorities expressed their frustration to the investigators from New York. They did not understand why the information and photos of Faiello were not sent to them sooner. They could have commenced the search days earlier if they had been better informed of the situation.

In no time, though, they ferreted out an important detail. The passport Dean used to enter the country had not been shown at any exit point. Dean was, in all likelihood, still within the borders of Costa Rica. His three-month visa had expired in December. He could easily be picked up and held on a visa violation while other charges were investigated.

Together the two governments issued an all points bulletin. Newspapers published in English and in Spanish splashed Dean's face across the country. Financial specialists tracked Dean's credit card usage. The net tightened as the unsuspecting Dean lounged by the pool. Diplomatic security special agents assigned to the United States Embassy in San Jose coordinated the search efforts of the various Costa Rican law enforcement agencies, and kept the New York authorities informed of developments.

At Villas Playa Samara, one of the resort security guards approached hotel manager Max Navarro with a newspaper. "Look, Max. Look at this. We have a criminal here in the hotel."

Those were not the words anyone in charge of a tropical getaway ever wanted to hear. Max stared at the photograph, hoping his employee was wrong. But he could not deny the evidence. On the front page he saw the unmistakable image of the customer staying in the three-bedroom villa—the man who loved to eat red snapper and always gave the bartenders good tips. It was not a good day for Max—and it was about to become an even worse one for Dean Faiello.

Max picked up the phone and called his wife at their home in the resort. "Don't leave the house. Lock the doors. We have a murderer here." After seeing to his family, Max performed his obligation as a law-abiding citizen—he called the police.

But Max's duty was not yet complete. Dean Faiello was still, after all, a guest at his resort. He called prominent criminal attorney Moises Vincenzi and said, "I have a guy here at the Villa who is going to need a lawyer right away."

Vincenzi hopped on a plane and flew straight to the airport nearest the resort.

With Max's call to the police, the Costa Rican immigration agency was notified. Special Officer Roger Morales and a handful of his colleagues rushed to Villas Playa Samara. They found Dean stretched out on a poolside chaise with an icy Corona in his hand—and attorney Moises Vincenzi at his side.

When Dean saw the approaching force of immigration police, one Interpol agent and six officers of Organismo de Investigacion Judicial—the highest ranking of the six branches of the Costa Rican police force—the vacationing fugitive jumped to his feet. He raised both hands up in the air, saying, "Take it easy. No problem."

Morales pulled out his handcuffs. Dean asked if he could change out of his bathing suit and slug back one last big glass of vodka. He was escorted to his villa to change into street clothes—but no one was serving any drinks.

Vincenzi insisted, to authorities and to the media, that Dean was nothing more than a tourist, and had no idea that police were looking for him.

The Department of Foreign Affairs wasted no time in voicing their pleasure at Dean Faiello's capture. "I praise the police authorities involved in the arrest of the suspect responsible for Cruz's death," Secretary Delia Domingo Albert said. "Let us hope that this will result in justice being served for Cruz's family. I have instructed Ambassador Albert Del Rosario in Washington to keep us informed on the case and to provide assistance to Cruz's family should they require it."

Understandably, the Cruz family expressed their feelings in far less diplomatic language. Irenea Cruz said, "He is crazy, mentally sick. It's inhumane what he did. My daughter was murdered. Why did he do this? I want the death penalty."

Rudolfo said, "When I saw him on TV during his arrest, I got so mad that my body started shaking." Then he echoed his wife's sentiments. "We want the death penalty! He deserves capital punishment. If I could speak to him face-to-face, I would tell him to go to hell—that's the best place for him. Why did he kill my daughter? How could he do it?"

Although their words expressed anger, their spirits were somewhat soothed by the arrest. Since the discovery of their daughter's body a week ago, they could hardly rest. Now, they felt some relief from their pain; and with that small measure of peace, sleep came at last.

CHAPTER THIRTY-THREE

JEANE'S CELL PHONE CHIRPED. IT WAS MARCO BADILLA. "They picked him up. They're going to bring him to jail in San Jose."

"When?" Jeane asked.

"They said very late—under the cover of the night."

"It sure would be nice to get pictures, Marco," Jeane said. Then she explained the concept of the traditional perp walk in the United States.

"I'll see what I can do," Marco said.

Whatever he did, it worked. Police loaded Dean Faiello into a red police pick-up truck at the Villa. His official escort, Marco Badilla, transported him down the primitive system of roads that led to San Jose. Dean's lawyer Moises Vincenzi flew back to the capital to await his client's arrival.

Director Badilla delivered Dean to authorities in San Jose at 7:30 that night. He parked on Main Street so Dean had to make a handcuffed walk, giving reporters plenty of opportunity for photographs and video footage.

Outside the jail, MacIntosh found that she was no longer the lone reporter in Costa Rica covering Dean's case. A crowd of fifty international news people—predominately New York–area print and broadcast journalists—surrounded the path from the vehicle to the immigration jail, shooting video, snapping still shots and peppering the air with questions.

In the crowd, Dean spotted Investigator Brian Ford. "Hi, Brian. Nice to see a familiar face." The line sounded as if it belonged to Leonardo DiCaprio's character as he greeted Tom Hanks in *Catch Me If You Can*—one of Dean's favorite films.

Attorney Vincenzi arrived at the immigration jail with a sack from Burger King containing a hamburger and a Coke. To the media, he repeated that Dean was nothing more than a tourist who had no idea that the police were looking for him. Vincenzi then took the meal inside to his client.

After Dean finished eating, the two men entered an interrogation room with Ford and Buffolino from the New York state attorney general's office and Detectives Della Rocca and Jennings from the Homicide Unit at the New York Police Department. Dean greeted Brian and Joe by their first names and asked how they were doing. He was his usual charming self. Despite their natural reluctance, the investigators found Dean quite likeable. Brian Ford later said, "For a murder suspect, he's really a nice guy."

In addition to posing questions that Dean's lawyer would not let him answer, the four men tried to persuade Dean not to fight extradition. They argued for the better conditions and better food in American prisons. Dean was obstinate in his desire to stay in Costa Rica. Then they dangled the possibility of visits from his sister Debra as bait. That argument resonated with Dean. "Let me sleep on it," he said.

Dean spent most of that night in the immigration jail crying. He was too distressed to notice how lucky he was. The other forty-nine inhabitants of the prison were crowded into one large cage, containing only six bunks. Dean had a cell to himself.

◆ ◆ ◆

TO NO ONE'S GREAT SURPRISE, THE ONE REPORTER WHO MANaged to get an interview with Faiello was Jeane MacIntosh. At 6 the next morning, Jeane's phone rang. On the other end, someone spoke in rapid-fire Spanish. She shouted, "*Un momento. Un momento*," then raced to Bolivar's room. She woke him up and put him on the line.

Jeane fidgeted as Bolivar talked to the caller. When he hung up, he told her, "They said you need to hurry over to the jail right now if you want to get in. They can't promise that he'll talk to you, but if you come right away, they will let you in."

Jeane rushed out of the hotel still wearing her pajama bottoms. She entered through the back door and was escorted to the jail's interrogation room. Dean came in wearing a scruffy sky-blue Hawaiian shirt, a pair of flipflops, handcuffs and a smile. "Hello, Jeane. How are you?"

"Dean, every time I see you, you're in handcuffs."

"We have to stop meeting like this," he joked. As always when they talked, Dean focused his eyes on her as if she were the only person of interest in the whole world. For twenty minutes, he sang Costa Rica's praises. He told her how much he enjoyed the social scene in San Jose's gay community and the coastal beauty of the country. "Costa Rican beaches are an unspoiled paradise. You can walk for miles and not see anyone," he said. "And I took a lot of long walks and saw a lot of sunrises and sunsets. The sunsets here are unlike any in the world."

"I've been in San Jose the whole time, running around, looking for you," Jeane said.

"You should have known I was at the beach," Dean said with a laugh.

When Jeane asked him about Maria Cruz, his constant gaze moved from her face, and he turned his head to the side. He would not look at her until she changed the subject.

Dean asked for a glass of milk and as he drank it, they continued to chat. "Did you dance at Pucho's?" Jeane asked.

"Sure, I danced at the club."

"Why, Dean?"

"Because it's fun. I love to dance. You should try it."

"I mean, were you hired there as a go-go dancer?"

Dean laughed.

"A lady at Pucho's told me she hired you. Is that true?"

"I love to dance, Jeane."

"But as a go-go dancer, Dean? You're forty years old."

Dean just smiled—vanity gleamed bright in his eyes.

She asked him about the body discovered in his Newark home and he turned away again. He said, "You'll have to speak to my attorney about all of that."

He did talk openly, though, about his fear. "I'm scared to death," he said. What frightened him the most was the possibility that he would never see his sister again. "I'm worried for myself, but more concerned about what my sister and friends are dealing with. All I can say is, send my love to my sister."

He spoke, too, about his surprise at being discovered so quickly by the authorities and about his lack of awareness that a search was underway. "I had no idea. I did not know until I spoke with my lawyer what was going on," he said. "Nobody called me. Phones in Costa Rica are a luxury. I don't watch TV."

"Do you have anything to say to the family of Maria Cruz?" MacIntosh asked.

Dean stared straight ahead. The expression on his face did not waver. It remained rigid and blank. He did not utter a word.

Officers entered the room and told Jeane her time was

up. She left out a side door and snuck away to her hotel. There, she slipped out of her pajamas and donned normal work attire. She then joined the media crowd at the jail. Reporters who knew her welcomed her, asking if she'd overslept. Had she been in the jail? they asked. She avoided answering, admitting the truth only to one persistent colleague.

BACK ON THE COAST, MAX NAVARRO AND HIS STAFF WORKED TO return the Villas Playa Samara to normal. They cleaned and prepared the three-bedroom villa for new guests. In the process, they came across an item overlooked by the police, who had searched there the day before. To their surprise, law enforcement had left behind a brown leather bag that looked like something a doctor would carry on house visits.

Opening it, they found a Baggie full of marijuana, a half-smoked joint, glassine envelopes of heroin, boxes of Gas-X, an assortment of skin care products and a paper money wrap that contained $5,000 in $100 bills. Max turned his find over to authorities.

DEAN FACED ARRAIGNMENT ON AN EXTRADITION WARRANT that named him as a suspect in the death of Maria Cruz without detailing any of the precise charges against him. After this hearing, Dean was moved to the regular jail on Avenida Primera—First Avenue. His new home was a run-down, overcrowded prison built for a maximum occupancy of 2,000, but now crawling with significantly more.

He moved into a cell with thirty-four other inmates, where he would remain, at least until New York authorities formalized the charges against him. The clock was ticking—New York had sixty days to deliver.

CHAPTER THIRTY-FOUR

AS SOON AS PATTY ROSADO HEARD OF DEAN'S ARREST, SHE called the offices of legendary defense attorney Johnnie Cochran. He'd become a household name in 1994 when football hero O. J. Simpson, charged with the murder of his ex-wife Nicole Brown Simpson and her acquaintance Ron Goldman, hired Cochran to defend him. Cochran and the Dream Team succeeded in keeping O.J. out of jail.

If Cochran could get a not guilty verdict for Simpson, Patty figured, surely he could do the same for Dean. Then she learned that the first one-hour consultation with the esteemed attorney required a $10,000 payment up front. She begged off.

IN THE AFTERMATH OF DEAN'S ARREST, MORE THAN A FEW people paid for their roles in helping him follow his road to perdition. The Office of Professional Discipline at the state department of education turned over to the department of health a list of doctors they suspected of enabling Dean's medical practice. Investigators in the health department sought to determine if any of them had provided Dean with prescriptions or pharmaceuticals.

Some suffered through the hassle of an inquiry, coming out the other side unscathed. Two physicians, however, took a fall for their ethical compromises in aiding Dean Faiello.

The New York State Office of Professional Medical Conduct charged Andrew Reyner, M.D., a psychiatrist specializing in psychopharmacology, with forty-five specifications of medical misconduct. Between February of 1998 and November of 2001, he prescribed and provided bulk quantities of Stadol; antibiotics erythromycin and aveloz; temazepam, a sedative hypnotic used to relieve insomnia; the anti-depressant BuSpar; the anti-anxiety drug Ativan; and the erectile dysfunction drug Viagra to Dean Faiello without obtaining adequate medical history, performing a physical examination or making a diagnosis. He did this, they charged, knowing that Faiello had a history of substance abuse and dependence, and a record for forging prescriptions.

The board cited Reyner for prescribing drugs to fourteen of Dean's customers, again without examination or diagnosis. They claimed he'd told investigators in November 2003 that he was with Faiello at a conference in Reno, Nevada, when he prescribed Stadol for him—then, in March 2004, told them that he was not with Dean in Reno. The Office of Professional Medical Conduct did not know which version was true, but they knew that he'd lied on one of the two occasions.

In November 2004, after more than eighteen years of practicing medicine in the state of New York, Andrew Reyner signed a consent agreement allowing authorities to suspend his license for four years. He now had to close his medical practice. Within fifteen days of the December 20 effective date, he would need to notify all of his active patients in writing of his suspension and provide referrals to another physician.

He had to inform the Drug Enforcement Agency

(DEA) of his loss of license and turn over the DEA certificate that allowed him to prescribe controlled substances. He had to return any unused prescription forms to the Bureau of Controlled Substances at the New York Health Department. Reyner could not accept any money for professional services or consultations and could not occupy space in any office where someone with a medical license provided health care services.

If he violated any of these provisions, he would be subject to civil and criminal penalties. In December 2008, he would be eligible for his license, but only if he could demonstrate to the Committee of Professional Conduct that he was fit and competent to practice medicine. To do that, he needed to pass a clinical competency assessment, and enroll in a course of personalized continuing medical education and in another program on ethics.

Once Reyner fulfilled those requirements, he would have his license returned, but would face an eight-year probationary period under the supervision of a monitoring physician. His license, however, would be permanently limited. Andrew Reyner could never prescribe medications to any patient in New York again.

In 2006, Andrew Reyner worked as a clinical instructor of psychiatry at the Mount Sinai School of Medicine.

THE NEXT TO FALL WAS MICHAEL JACKOWITZ, D.O., THE ONE-time house physician for the New York City Ballet and the Metropolitan Opera, and another designated medical director for SkinOvations. This doctor of osteopathy was a member of Physician Volunteers for the Arts in Manhattan. He also was active in the theater itself, having graduated from the Commercial Theater Institute in 1996.

In 1997 he formed MJM Productions with Josephine Abrady and Marvin Kahan and produced off-Broadway and regional shows, including Nicky Silver's *The Food*

Chain at the Westside Theatre. He was also involved in the Broadway production of *Flower Drum Song* and Sarah Jones' one-woman show, *bridge & tunnel*, produced by Meryl Streep.

By the time New York authorities came knocking, Jackowitz no longer resided in New York. He had moved to Santa Barbara, California, and immersed himself in theater there. When they caught up with him, he was preparing for a production of *tick . . . tick . . . BOOM!* scheduled to open as the first performance in the 2005–2006 season of the Rubicon Theatre, a non-profit regional theater in the Downtown Cultural District of Ventura.

Officials charged Jackowitz with prescribing Viagra and the sleeping aid Sonata to Dean Faiello between June 2001 and August 2002. Additionally, they claimed he had written prescriptions for Stadol, Ativan, the antibiotic doxycycline and Vioxx—a drug for the treatment of osteoarthritis—for twenty-five of Dean's clients without performing a physical examination or even informing the patients that prescriptions had been issued in their names.

The accusations continued, stating that Jackowitz knew Dean would use some of these drugs in the performance of laser hair removal, laser face resurfacing, mole removal, spider vein removal, tattoo removal and scar revision, without the adequate supervision of a physician.

They alleged that Jackowitz also gave signed prescription pads to Dean Faiello with the patient name and drug name left blank for Dean to fill out as he pleased. They had proof that he accepted money from Dean in return for his services and for serving as the nominal medical director of SkinOvations.

The state Office of Professional Medical Conduct ruled that Jackowitz was guilty of negligence and gross negligence, incompetence and gross incompetence, aiding and abetting an unlicensed person, fraud and moral unfitness to practice medicine. In January 2005, he signed a consent agreement, accepting a one-year suspension of his medical license and a three-year probationary period after regaining it. The terms of his suspension and probation were the same as those imposed on Andrew Reyner with one exception. When Jackowitz reclaimed his license, he would be able to get a DEA certificate and resume writing prescriptions.

He submitted an application for an osteopathic Physicians and Surgeons Certificate in July 2004, to the Osteopathic Medical Board of California. He swore to the truthfulness of all the statements he made in the document, but the reviewing body suspected he was not completely open or honest. After an investigation, the board denied Jackowitz a license to practice, based on the disciplinary action taken in New York. They also billed him for the costs of their investigation.

In the summer of 2006, Michael Jackowitz was in California involved in a number of television and theater projects. He'd begun work on his most ambitious project to date—the development of a world premiere opera by award-winning composer Stephen Schwartz, planned to open for Opera Santa Barbara in 2009.

LAW ENFORCEMENT IN TWO STATES FOCUSED IN ON DEAN'S sister, Debra. One of Dean's Newark neighbors told police that Debra and Patty removed Dean's patient files and a bag of possessions from his room at Mark Ritchey's place. It was reported that the bag contained Maria's identification, keys and credit cards.

They knew Debra picked up Dean's Jeep Cherokee from the New Jersey impound lot—the same SUV Dean used to transport Maria's body from Manhattan to Newark. They knew she went by Ritchey's place and got the title to the vehicle and transferred the ownership into her name. The question was, had she done anything with the intention of covering Dean's tracks?

The New Jersey State Police department of Internal Affairs began an investigation. One of the people they called was Jeane MacIntosh. They wanted to know where she got information about Dean's Jeep, the electronic money transfer and anything else connected to Debra Faiello for her published stories. "My source contacted another reporter," she said. "Brad Hamilton received the phone call . . . I cannot reveal another reporter's sources."

Internal Affairs contacted Brad, but he disappointed them, too. He refused to divulge his source. A spokesman for the New Jersey Police Department assured the media that Sergeant Faiello was cooperating with the investigation in every way she could.

Many observers of the department were skeptical. Suspicion that the troopers were once again protecting one of their own ran rampant. At the end of 1999, the United States Justice Department determined that a monitor needed to be appointed by a federal judge to provide oversight of the New Jersey Police Department, after discrimination and racial profiling were found to be pervasive. Federal authorities also accorded the monitor the responsibility of overseeing a dramatic reorganization in the Internal Affairs office, inspired by a long history of accusations of cronyism and cover-up.

The monitor could demand a reinvestigation if the findings or techniques employed in an Internal Affairs investigation appeared at all suspicious. Many—including attorney Tom Shanahan—thought the feds should investigate the conduct of the police in their probe into Debra Faiello's actions.

The New Jersey police were not sharing their findings with the media, and appeared disinterested in disciplining Debra. The district attorney's office in Manhattan, though, had serious concerns about her involvement in her brother's case. They launched a criminal investigation of their own.

CHAPTER THIRTY-FIVE

IF ONE OF DEAN'S INNER CIRCLE HAD NOT STEPPED FORWARD with an essential bit of information, authorities would not have known to look in Newark, and the body of Maria Cruz might still be under that slab of concrete in the carriage house. A lot of people possessed a small piece of the puzzle of Maria's disappearance, but it was Greg who made the initial contact with Investigator Ford in the attorney general's office. Without his honesty, Maria's family still might not know what happened to their beloved Ate Pipay. The answers they now had were dreadful and tragic; but at least the family no longer faced the anguish of not knowing.

Greg knew that he did not speak up to authorities out of malice toward Dean. He'd acted because it was the right thing to do. Still, the tabloid press labeled him as a vindictive ex-lover, a vengeful paramour and worse. Their descriptions saddened Greg, but his concern about that matter paled in comparison to his distress over the growing skepticism of the authorities. In a meeting with Detective Della Rocca and Assistant District Attorney Ann Prunty, it demonstrated itself.

Records from the telephone in his apartment were slapped on the table. Della Rocca pointed to a number of calls made to drug dealers who provided a home delivery service. Greg was furious that Dean used his phone to call dealers, and further outraged that he had illegal drugs delivered to Greg's home. He told Della Rocca and Prunty just that. They, however, accused him of being involved in drugs, too.

Della Rocca pointed out in his phone records the night Maria died, "You called Patty Rosado that night."

"I did?"

"Yes. You talked to her for fifteen minutes."

Greg saw the proof before his eyes, but he certainly did not remember the call.

"What did you two talk about?"

"I don't know. I don't remember anything special that night. It was just an ordinary evening."

A look of disgust crossed Della Rocca's face, his disbelief apparent. Then the detective pointed to the call Greg made right after talking to Patty. "What did you talk to this guy about?"

"I don't recall. He's my best friend. We talked. I don't remember the conversation. As I said, it was not a memorable night for me."

"There's another thing that bothers me, Bach. We have the phone records from Carl James' apartment. There was no call from there to Martin Mannert that night."

"There wasn't?"

"No. Why would someone in a trauma situation call their accountant, anyway?" Della Rocca asked.

"I don't know. I just know what Martin told me."

"Would you call an accountant if somebody was dying?"

Greg did not answer. He did not know what to say.

Then they questioned Greg about the first call he made the morning after Maria's death. "That's a lawyer's office. Why did you call your attorney *that* morning, Mr. Bach?"

"That's the lawyer who wrote up the promissory note

regarding the money Dean owed me. I called him for advice about that."

"Really?"

"Yes."

"You called him *that* morning about money?" Skepticism put an ugly edge on Della Rocca's voice.

Greg repeated his answer, but realized that no matter what he said or how many times he said it, they were not going to believe him. He signed a document waiving his attorney–client privilege so his lawyer could answer the investigators' questions. Greg hoped they would believe his attorney. However, neither Prunty nor Della Rocca ever made that follow-up call.

Greg left the meeting in turmoil, wondering if what they had told him was even true. *Did Della Rocca make some of that stuff up?* he wondered. Greg knew he could no longer trust the investigators or the prosecutors.

Greg took the tone of the meeting as an indication that he needed a criminal attorney on his side, but he didn't want to go into further debt hiring one. Dean trashed his credit and left him in a deep financial hole—he was already climbing as fast as he could, and there was no end in sight.

He sought legal advice elsewhere. First, Greg visited the Legal Aid Society of New York. Since he was not charged with a crime, though, they could not help him. He then consulted with advisors at the Lambda Legal Defense and Education Fund. Greg, however, had no reason to believe he was being discriminated against because of his sexual preferences. The Gay/Lesbian Center sponsored a legal clinic each month in which they offered free fifteen-minute consultations with attorneys. Greg made an appointment. It would be difficult to condense his bizarre story into the short time frame allotted, and revealing it was embarrassing. But he did it anyway.

"It looks like you've gotten yourself into a sticky wicket," the lawyer said, but aside from that observation, offered nothing more.

Up until this point, Greg avoided interviews with the media. He didn't want his role in the mystery exposed. He didn't want Dean to know that he went to the police. But the tabloids outed him just the same, and they did it in what he regarded as a sleazy, nasty way.

Greg wanted to counteract the negative effects of the stories. He needed to talk to someone who might give him answers—information about the chain of events that he had not been able to get from the police. And he hoped that if he told his whole story to a reputable publication, everyone would read it and at last leave him alone.

Greg chose to approach *Vanity Fair* first. He selected them because of their reputation for journalistic integrity. He knew there were less reputable venues out there who would pay him for his story, but Greg was more interested in enhancing his credibility than in lining his pocket. Walking into their offices on the seventh floor of 4 Times Square, he asked if they were interested. They were, and they assigned Bryan Burrough to cover the story. Greg told him about his involvement in Dean's life and the recovery of Maria's body. But Bryan could not offer him any new information—he knew less than Greg. He suggested that Greg contact the producers at *48 Hours*.

The CBS show began covering the disappearance of Maria Cruz in the summer of 2003 as part of a bigger story about missing persons in New York. At some point, the story seemed to be going nowhere, so they shelved their footage and let it drop. But new developments in the Maria Cruz case revitalized their interest, and they resurrected the material.

Greg approached the producers with great trepidation. It was a big stretch for a private person like him. Again, Greg divulged his story to a media outlet whose policy prohibited paying for interviews. But the *48 Hours*–Greg Bach collaboration proved mutually beneficial in other ways. Greg filled in some blanks for Harold Dow, one of the show's star producers, and field producer Susan Mallie, and they answered many of Greg's questions in return.

Again and again, Greg fielded queries about the $25,000 reward money. Why hadn't he requested it? Initially, Greg had seen the fund as blood money, and wanted nothing to do with it. But as time went by, his attitude changed. He suffered a lot of inconvenience by coming forward, and he staggered under the financial burden of Dean's actions. He decided in the end to request the reward.

First, he called CrimeStoppers. They said that the reward was not listed with them. He needed to call Detective Della Rocca they told him. Greg thought about it for a few days before he got up the nerve to call the detective and ask about it.

"We want to wait until Dean is in the United States before we deal with that," Della Rocca responded.

But the people at *48 Hours* insisted that he was entitled to the money and that he should contact Barclays—after all, they put up half of the money, and should have some control over the distribution. Greg discussed the issue with the human resources department at Barclays, who also referred him to Della Rocca.

Greg called the detective again and pointed out that the reward was not offered for the return of Dean Faiello but for information leading to the whereabouts of Maria Cruz.

"That's not what I do," Della Rocca said. "Call th number on the poster."

"Your number is on the poster, Detective. That's why am calling you."

Greg did not understand. He had cooperated full from the beginning. He never even got a thank you, onl grief.

The next time Greg met with Assistant District Attor ney Ann Prunty and Detective Della Rocca, their hostilit sucked the air out of the room. They peppered him wit questions that sounded very familiar to Greg. "Are yo asking me about stuff you read in the *Vanity Fair* articl or what's in police reports?"

He got no answer, but knew his assumption was right Still, it made no sense.

Referring to the death of Maria Cruz and the disposa of her body, Della Rocca asked, "You mean you're tellin me you didn't know?"

"That's exactly what I've been telling you from the be ginning, Detective," Greg said.

"We believe you knew all about it, Mr. Bach. If we'r right, we'll charge you with conspiracy after the fact," Prunty said.

"I did nothing wrong. I brought my suspicions to In vestigator Ford. I didn't know if they were justified or not You know there's no truth to that charge."

Prunty ignored Greg's assertions of innocence and lef him feeling that she did not care.

Greg left the encounter stunned. Anger roiled throug his body. First Dean used him and tossed him aside. Nov the authorities were doing the same thing. Greg could no worry about the expense any longer. He needed a crimi nal attorney. He hired one that day.

With that action, Greg severed the line of direct com munication between himself and the investigation o

Dean Faiello. Greg would no longer speak to investigators without his attorney present. After all of his cooperation, it galled Greg to think that any time he sat down with the authorities, he would have to pay a legal fee. Unfortunately, he felt he had no other choice.

CHAPTER THIRTY-SIX

AFTER DEAN MOVED OUT OF THE IMMIGRATION FACILITY AND into the regular jail, most of the reporters headed back home. Jeane MacIntosh stuck around. She was there on March 17, 2004, when the office of Manhattan District Attorney Robert M. Morganthau filed a felony arrest warrant with the Criminal Court of the City of New York charging Dean Faiello with one count of murder in the second degree:

> The defendant, under circumstances evincing a depraved indifference to human life, recklessly engaged in conduct which created a grave risk of death to another person, and thereby caused the death of another person.

Two circumstances allowed the district attorney to charge Dean with murder instead of manslaughter, even though when Dean injected the lidocaine into the tongue of Maria Cruz, he had no intention of killing her or doing her any harm. First of all, Maria's death occurred in the commission of another crime—practicing medicine without a license. Second, Dean called Dr. Goldschmitt who'd advised him to rush Maria to the hospital. Dean chose to ignore the advice that could have saved Maria's life.

When Dean fled from the United States, he faced a 6-month term of imprisonment. With these new charges, he now looked at the possibility of 25 years to life behind bars.

BEFORE RETURNING TO NEW YORK, JEANE MACINTOSH received an invitation to dinner with Costa Rican defense attorney Moises Vincenzi, at his home in the country. Vincenzi had a long history of death threats, compelling him to wear a bullet-proof vest and travel with armed guards. Knowing this, Jeane was not surprised to discover that Vincenzi lived in a gated community and had armed guards around the perimeter of the home where he lived with his beautiful wife and son.

After a pleasant dinner, Jeane was taking her leave when she tripped over a suitcase standing behind a sofa. She righted it and noticed an identification tag labeling it as the property of Dean Faiello. "Can I look inside?" she asked.

Vincenzi rushed over to secure the bag. "I've been storing some of Dean's belongings for him."

"Come on, let me take a peek inside. Have you looked at the contents? Maybe there's another body in there," she joked.

Vincenzi laughed. "Maybe so," he said, but he would not let Jeane check it out.

MOISES VINCENZI CONTINUED HIS BATTLE WITH THE POWER vested in the New York government. Most extradition requests resulted in the fugitive's return within six months of arrest. But, thanks to Vincenzi, six months after Dean's capture, he remained in San Jose.

Somehow, Dean arranged for take-out meals from McDonald's, Burger King and Pizza Hut to supplement the usual prison fare of beans and rice and had money placed into the accounts of other inmates to provide protection for him behind bars. In addition, he paid a lot of money to jailers to enjoy the simple luxury of sleeping on a bed each night. In the first six months of his incarceration in Costa Rica, $7,000 went through Dean's hands to pay for these perks.

Vincenzi denied that he'd made these arrangements. "It was my job to protect him legally, not in jail. It is not my business what he does in jail. I did not get into those issues with him."

Dean expected Vincenzi to get him out of jail while he awaited a decision on the extradition request. Vincenzi tried, petitioning the judge to allow his client to go to his beach home and report in to court every two weeks. His request was denied.

When it appeared that Vincenzi had exhausted his arsenal of maneuvers to delay extradition, Dean fired him. He knew that changing lawyers would automatically delay the legal process a little bit longer. "Dean Faiello thinks he can buy liberty," a Costa Rican lawyer told Jeane MacIntosh. "But Vincenzi doesn't operate that way. He believes in the justice process. If Faiello had had a bad defense, he'd be back in the United States already."

"The guy's a fool," Vincenzi said. "He won't listen to anyone. He prefers living in a Costa Rican jail to coming back to the States." Vincenzi could not understand how Dean—or anyone—would choose the primitive conditions of the Central American jail over the far more civilized situation in U.S. prisons.

DEAN FOUGHT EXTRADITION TO THE UNITED STATES IN THE San Sebastian jail with 1,200 inmates awaiting trial. Because of the facility's high elevation, he often watched clouds drifting through the grounds. During the wet season, heavy rains pounded down on the corrugated roof of the jail, creating a loud—but oddly soothing—drumming noise. "I found it very peaceful to read in the library and hear and feel the rain," Dean wrote. "The noise from the rain also cancelled out a lot of the cacophony of jail noises such as prisoners shouting and the metal clanging of gates."

Dean caught exotic glimpses of volcanoes and the surrounding lush rainforests from many parts of the jail, but his favorite spot was the path to the attorney meeting room in an adjacent building. To reach it, Dean walked through an outdoor garden filled with hanging pendulas, banana trees, bougainvillea, palm trees and marble statues of saints. While waiting outside for his lawyer to finish up with other inmate-clients, Dean spent time reading and admiring the flowers in that serene oasis.

After his meeting, he returned to the chaos of his dormitory-style unit. There, a group of fifty-five men shared two toilets, two showers and one sink. There were no electrical outlets, no hot water and lights were turned on for only four hours a day from 6 to 10 P.M.

Pandemonium reigned over the area until midnight. Then, for a few hours, a restless near-quiet descended over the unit, broken only by coughing, sneezing and hacking. Half of the men slept on uncomfortable cots and the other half curled up on the floor.

The government of Costa Rica provides medical care, prescriptions and surgery to all of its citizens at no charge, but the wait for services is often long for everyone. Jail was no exception. Dean often had to wait two to three weeks just to see the doctor. Then, he found that the government did not provide any HIV medications to prisoners. Dean's T-cell count plummeted from 420 to 183. His viral load shot up from undetectable levels to over 16,000. He contracted pneumocystis carinii, the most common opportunistic infection in people with HIV, and cytomegalovirus, a naturally occurring virus that rarely causes illness except among those like Dean whose immune systems were compromised.

Another drawback to the jail was the food. There were only two meals a day: lunch and dinner. For both meals, the menu was the same: black beans and rice. Occasionally, the rice was enlivened with bits of vegetable and ground beef, but that was as extravagant as it got. Inmates never received chicken or fish, bread, fruit, juice or dessert.

To make matters worse, every meal tasted of the scorched canola oil that was used again and again long past its prime. Despite occasional supplementary meals from the outside, Dean lost thirty pounds in the fifteen months he spent in the facility.

To get out of the dorm room, Dean taught English at the jail school five days a week for five to seven hours each day. "I was fortunate in that my students were very motivated," Dean wrote.

> Even though there were no officers in the classrooms, I never had a disciplinary problem. I think that had to do with the fact that the school offered so much. Those who caused trouble would miss out on the use of computers, painting classes, wood-working shop (yes, with power tools and cutting blades!), candle-making, sewing classes, watercolors and even free coffee, which was the real reason I stuck it out.

Dean took advantage of the prison library, stocked with hundreds of books in Spanish, German and English. He often selected a paperback novel in his native tongue, but also learned to read Spanish with a dictionary at his fingertips. Hemingway in Spanish was a pleasurable challenge for Dean. He read *Islas en el Golfo* (*Islands in the Stream*), *Por Quien Doblan las Campanas* (*For Whom the Bell Tolls*), and *El Viejo y el Mar* (*The Old Man and the Sea*). He also enjoyed the Spanish translations of J. R. R. Tolkien's books, but found that the works of Lillian Hellman fell flat in that language. Between this reading and learning to communicate with his fellow inmates, he was fluent in Spanish within months.

JEANE MACINTOSH RETURNED TO NEW YORK AND, WITH A PHOtographer, staked out the house of Dr. David Goldschmitt, awaiting his arrival from work. Once he returned, they gave him a few minutes, then knocked on the front door. David welcomed them inside.

Chaos ruled in the old Victorian home, where a major renovation was underway. David gave the *Post* duo a tour. They stepped over tools and lumber and dodged scaffolding as he explained the work in progress and the expected outcome. He told them about the history of his house, as well as that of Dean's place up the street.

He talked about his concerns for Dean. As a doctor, David knew all too well the risks faced by a bisexual who was promiscuous. "It made me crazy when he went cruising for guys." He said that Dean often went trolling in a seedy area near the neighborhood of Forest Hill.

He related the events of the night Maria died. "I could have saved her—somebody could have saved her if Dean had just called an ambulance. I tried desperately to make him understand she needed immediate medical attention. That's the worst part. In cases like this, we save ninety-five percent of them. It's very rare for someone to die, unless you wait too long for medical attention.

"He said she was a friend. Was that the truth? Now, I don't know. I've learned that Dean can be a very convincing liar."

Jeane asked to take a picture of him. He agreed, but excused himself first to don a fresh shirt. Jeane asked, "How do you feel now about what Dean has done?"

"I can't forgive him. He tortured this woman's family for ten months. I cannot imagine the anguish they went through. But maybe I might be able to give the family some comfort to know that she probably wasn't in pain when she died."

Before they left, David told them about his annual Christmas party and got their phone numbers so he could invite them to the next one.

FOR MONTHS, THE PRODUCERS OF *48 HOURS MYSTERY* NEGOTI-ated with Dean's attorneys for an interview. Finally, access was granted. Harold Dow and his crew flew to Costa Rica. They entered the crumbling, derelict building that housed prisoners in San Jose and immediately realized that conditions here were far more rustic than in any New York prison.

Dean started the conversation with complaints. His voice sounded whiny, but the expression on his face appeared arrogant. "The truth is, I'm very unhappy with my physical health at this point. It's no secret I'm HIV positive. I have been here for six months without any treatment, any medical treatment of my HIV condition. I think I've lost eleven kilos, which is about twenty-two pounds."

Dow's face bore the countenance of a placid pool. As a practiced interviewer and listener, he knew when it was in his best interest to conceal—or to reveal—any judgmental feelings toward his subject. He asked Dean why he continued to fight extradition when he faced such miserable living conditions.

Before answering, Dean darted his eyes sideways to his attorney, Nuria Mataritta Martinez. Then, in a seeming contradiction of his previous complaints, Dean said, "I like Costa Rica and I'm doing everything that I can with my attorney and in my legal powers to stay here in this country. I wish to spend the rest of my life here in Costa Rica."

Dean's new lawyer stood on the sidelines during the interview, interrupting whenever she did not want Dean to answer. She clearly harbored doubts about the wisdom of allowing CBS to speak with her client, and she tried to terminate the interview many times before she succeeded.

Dean, though, appeared to have a strong desire to tell his side of the story. Dow brushed aside the lawyer's interruptions, persisting with his customary tenacity: "Did you kill Maria Cruz?" he asked.

"I have no comment. I am innocent of the charges presented against me. I've been falsely accused by the U.S."

Dow raised his eyebrows in surprise. "You really feel you've been falsely accused by the United States?"

"Absolutely," Dean insisted.

Dow wanted to know why, if Dean was innocent, Maria's body was found in the garage of his Newark home.

"I have no statement about anything that happened in my house," Dean said.

"What would you want to say to Maria Cruz's family, if you are innocent?"

"I can't answer that."

"Are you concerned about these charges?"

Dean turned to his lawyer, whose agitation was quite obvious. He turned back to Dow. "My statement is, remains: I am innocent of the charges."

"Were you pretending to be a doctor in New York?"

"I have no comment on that," Dean said.

His attorney terminated the interview and removed Dean from the area.

IN DECEMBER OF 2004, A THREE-JUDGE PANEL CONVENED IN Costa Rica. They ruled that Dean Faiello could be extradited to the United States. Dean's new lawyer danced a legal tango, delaying her client's departure for five more months.

CHAPTER THIRTY-SEVEN

AFTER THE EPISODE OF *48 HOURS MYSTERY* ABOUT DEAN Faiello and Maria Cruz aired, Greg got a call from one of Oprah Winfrey's producers. She said, "Oprah thinks you are an interesting person with a fascinating story and would make a great guest on the show."

Greg rolled his eyes and turned down the request. *You know your relationship ended badly when Oprah calls*, he thought.

MEANWHILE, MARK AND PATTY'S RELATIONSHIP HAD GROWN more intense after Dean left the country. By May of 2005, though, they had a falling out. When he spoke to Greg Bach, Mark described her as "poisonous." Both men knew they'd been beguiled and manipulated by Dean's charm. Now Mark realized he had also been taken in by Patty.

LATE ON THURSDAY, MAY 19, 2005, JEANE MACINTOSH FIELDED A phone call from Monica Umana, a local reporter in San José. "They're extraditing Dean back to the States. He's not leaving tomorrow. It is unlikely that they'll transport him over the weekend. They'll probably fly him out on Monday."

Jeane called every official she knew involved in the

case, but no one in New York would confirm or deny the tip. She talked to her editors, who decided to fly her and photographer Josh Williams to Costa Rica. Their mission was clear: "Don't come back without a shot of Dean Faiello on the plane."

Jeane and Josh landed in San Jose on Sunday, May 22. The first order of business: Find out about all flights flying from Costa Rica to New Jersey or New York on Monday. They made a list, then attempted the decades-old reporter technique: Book seats on each and every flight to ensure you get on the right one.

Unfortunately, since 9-11, this method of covering all of the bases was no longer viable. Every time Jeane booked one flight, the previous one was automatically cancelled. She didn't realize that until she was a long way down her list.

She had to pick one flight and stick with it. *But which one?* she wondered. Jeane talked to employees at every relevant airline. They all assured her that there was a standard operating procedure employed by officials transporting a criminal. They always chose the flight closest to the hangar, where the wanted fugitives were brought when they entered the airport. Based on that, Jeane selected a Delta flight and chose two seats in different rows to increase the chances that one of them would get close to Faiello.

On Monday morning, Jeane and Josh hit the airport early. They had freelance reporters scattered in key locations. One staked out the jail. Another watched the highway to the airport. Jeane went to the counters of all the other airlines that had flights to New Jersey or New York and got their assurances that seats could be purchased for her and Josh at the last minute if the Delta gamble didn't pay off.

The first freelancer called in. "He's left the jail." Then

the second call arrived. "He's exiting the highway and heading for the airport."

Jeane and Josh positioned themselves in front of a large window overlooking the aircraft that awaited boarding. They looked in opposite directions, hoping to spot Dean the second he emerged from any of the buildings.

For thirty stressful minutes, they kept watch. Jeane second-guessed herself at least a dozen times. Then, there he was, walking out of the hangar the airport personnel indicated a day earlier. Surrounded by United States Marshals, he walked across the tarmac, up the stairs and into the Delta aircraft—the same flight Jeane had booked.

She and Josh rushed to the entrance ramp and boarded the plane. Jeane saw Dean sitting near the back in the middle seat with Marshals flanking him. Another Marshal sat in the row in front of him and yet another in the row behind. Jeane looked away quickly. She did not want to catch Dean's eye—not yet. And she didn't want to alert the Marshals to media presence on the plane.

Josh and Jeane took their seats and buckled up. After take-off, but before breakfast was served, Josh stepped in the aisle and walked past Jeane without looking in her direction. From the back of the plane, he snapped two quick photographs.

Jeane then heard a loud thump. She spun around only to find Josh flat on the aisle floor with two Marshals towering over him. Jeane swung back and faced front. She didn't want the agents to suspect that she was traveling with him.

As Josh remained on the floor, Jeane got antsy. She decided to walk to the back and go into the restroom, where she hoped she could eavesdrop on the Marshals. On her way down the aisle, she stepped over Josh, but she dared not look at him.

From the restroom Jeane overheard them telling Josh

that he would be arrested when the plane landed in Atlanta. She whipped out her cell phone and called New York to inform them of this latest development. She shut off her phone and exited the restroom. Josh was no longer on the floor as she returned to her seat, her heart racing.

While breakfast was being served, a thick folded-up piece of paper was nudged into her hand. She didn't dare look up to see who had put it there. Paranoia sent goose bumps racing up and down her arms and legs. She darted glances around the plane to make sure the Marshals were not watching her, then opened the note with slow deliberation. It was from Josh.

"Obviously, I've been made. Don't be connected to me. I may be arrested when we deplane in Atlanta." Inside the note was the digital memory card from Josh's camera. He managed to slip it out and tuck it away before the Marshals confiscated his camera. Jeane wrapped the paper back around the memory card and slid it into her purse. She tried to look like a normal passenger on a normal flight on a normal day. But inside she was terrified.

Dean watched the in-flight movie, *Ocean's Twelve*, and read the book he had brought along, *Split Second* by David Baldacci. Jeane, meanwhile, couldn't concentrate on anything.

At last, the flight landed in Atlanta. Jeane dawdled outside the gate waiting to see what would happen to Josh. The Marshals yelled warnings and threats at him, and when Josh agreed that he'd never do anything like that again, they returned his camera and released him.

Josh headed for the connecting flight. Jeane followed Dean and the Marshals to the gate, making sure she stayed out of Dean's line of sight. They all waited for forty-five minutes for boarding to begin for their flight to Newark.

Jeane was one of the first to take her assigned seat. It

was a middle seat in the back row. A Marshal approached her and said, "Ma'am, we're going to have to take your seat." He directed her to another just a couple of rows up and on the opposite side. From her new location, she had an excellent angle to keep her eye on Dean, as they positioned him in the seat she vacated.

Jeane kept a surreptitious watch on Dean throughout the flight. He read his book for most of it, but spent the last twenty minutes staring out the window, looking lost and forlorn. When the landing gear kissed the tarmac, he let out a huge sigh.

It came time to disembark, and Jeane acted is if she were having difficulties getting her belongings together. She delayed leaving her seat until nearly everyone else was off the plane. Then she walked back a couple of rows toward Dean.

He recognized her right away, pointing a finger at her and saying to the Marshals, "You should arrest her, too. She's with the media, too. She's with the *Post*."

One of the Marshals cast a dead look in her direction and asked who she was. Before she could respond, Dean interrupted. "Her name is Jeane MacIntosh. Arrest her."

"Dean, do you want to talk?" Jeane asked. "Do you want to say anything about your arrival back home?"

At the sound of her voice, Dean composed himself and donned a smile. "Do you have any plans for dinner tonight, Jeane?"

One of the Marshals pushed Jeane up the aisle and ushered her off the plane.

IN NEW YORK, MARSHALS TURNED CUSTODY OF THEIR PRISONER over to Investigators Brian Ford and Joe Buffolino of the attorney general's office. They escorted him to the Midtown North Precinct in Manhattan where they were joined by Detective Joe Della Rocca.

A media throng stood by, snapping pictures, shooting video and hoping for a comment from the elusive Faiello. Dean, though, wasn't talking. In a short-sleeved gray-striped button-down shirt, baggy blue jeans, alligator loafers and a pair of handcuffs, he looked at the ground, not making eye contact with anyone in the crowd. He appeared rumpled, tired, overly thin and in need of a shave. He didn't look capable of murder.

In Queens, Maria's Uncle Jose Navarro told reporters: "I'd like to thank the police department. They did a good job and I have faith in the justice system. I have faith in the district attorney's office."

Maria's father, at home near Manila in the Philippines, said, "Our prayers have been answered. If only our prayers could bring back Maria."

THE NEXT DAY, DEAN APPEARED BEFORE STATE SUPREME COURT Justice Gregory Carro for arraignment on the bail-jumping charge in connection with his unlicensed practice of medicine conviction. Defense Attorney Aaron Goldsmith, a lawyer in Margaret Shalley's firm, was by his side providing legal counsel.

Deciding that Dean was a flight risk was a no-brainer. "At this point, the defendant has already demonstrated a willingness not to return to court," the judge said as he denied Faiello's request for bail. He ordered Dean to return to court on June 13 for sentencing on the medical fraud charge—an inevitability he'd avoided for nearly two years. Instead of the 6 months of incarceration that Margaret Shalley negotiated for him before his flight to Costa Rica, Dean was now expected to receive the maximum sentence of 4 years.

CHAPTER THIRTY-EIGHT

DEAN APPEARED IN A COURTROOM AGAIN THAT THURSDAY—this time in Manhattan Criminal Court before Judge Anthony Ferrera—where he was arraigned for the first time on second-degree murder charges in the death of Maria Cruz. It was Dean's first encounter with the woman determined to put him behind bars for a long time: New York County Assistant District Attorney Ann Prunty.

Prunty was admitted to the New York Bar in 1985 and joined the trial division of the prosecutor's office.

She made her mark in the prosecutor's office in the summer of 1993 when she was appointed deputy bureau chief and volunteered for Project Octopus, an experimental effort to allow prosecutors a more proactive role in the fight against crime. Her laboratory was the Ninth Precinct on the Lower East Side, where the sidewalks were stained with a long history of drug violence.

Prunty set two goals for the initial phase of the project. First, educate her teams about the nature of criminal activity in the area. Secondly, develop the necessary relationships with precinct and housing authority police, and within the community itself, to create a smooth exchange of information and intelligence.

In a couple of months, Prunty developed the strategic

direction for the project. She forged a sustained, coordinated organizational arrangement between the attorneys and the police. By the end of 1994, the results of her efforts were apparent. Arrests of two-bit offenders—known as Dixie cups in the drug world for their easy disposability—had led to the arrest and conviction of more heavy-weight players in the narcotics trade.

Prunty's tenacity and resourcefulness were a proven commodity. She gained the grade of senior trial counsel and was assigned for a time to the Rackets Bureau. Her latest assignment: the Cold Case Unit of the trials division, where she brought her talents and experience to bear in her prosecution of Dean Faiello.

That morning in Judge Ferrera's court, Prunty announced her plans to present the case to the grand jury for a determination of the charges her office would be filing against the defendant. The judge denied bail and set the next court date for June 28.

Dean, meanwhile, had a new high-powered defense attorney by his side—Anthony Ricco. After the court session, Ricco told reporters, "This case, although there was a terrible loss of life, doesn't amount to a murder." He contemplated allowing Dean to testify before the grand jury, to get the charges reduced. "My client never intended to kill anyone."

When asked if Faiello's run to Costa Rica was an acknowledgment of guilt, Ricco said that it was more like panic. "One cannot determine guilt from flight. One runs from things, one runs to things," he said.

The reporters then asked him about Dean's prospects for conviction. "I always have an uphill battle," he said. "But I've learned in the long run that you have to reserve judgment. He's entitled to the presumption of innocence. It looks like a long road, but we've been on a long road

before. Oftentimes things are not what they appear to b
when all is said and done."

Anthony—Tony—Ricco with his rangy six-foot frame
bow-tied neck, jutting chin, shaved head and knack fo
story-telling, captivated every courtroom he entered. Bu
he began his life far lower on the socio-economic ladder.

Tony grew up with six siblings in Harlem on Wes
122nd Street in a neighborhood where pessimism thrivec
along with a never-ending supply of illegal drugs. He wa
just 9 years old in 1966 when the integration of the publi
schools swept him from his shabby world into a place o
privilege, one he didn't know existed. Bused to a schoc
on East 57th Street, he entered a world of white.

Tony's mother worked for the postal service for a goo
part of her life. His father was a bitter man, thwarted i
his choice of career because of the color of his skin. H
clung to a tattered letter he received in 1949 from NBC
radio. In it they informed him that it was against their po
icy to hire "colored men" as radio announcers.

Not all of Tony's siblings made it to adulthood. Whe
Tony was 12, his 15-year-old sister Marcia died of
heroin overdose in the bathtub of a ratty basement apart
ment.

After graduating from law school at Northeastern Uni
versity in Boston, Tony returned to New York and was ad
mitted to the bar in 1981. After a short time in the publi
sector, he set up a solo criminal law practice. In an articl
published in *New York* magazine, Deborah Plotz-Pierce
one of Ricco's elementary school teachers, told Chri
Smith, "I don't think he's attracted to lost causes. I thin
he goes after lost people, because in his family, he wa
surrounded by lost people. He couldn't help them then
but he can help others now."

Ricco made it his mission to champion those whom n
one else wanted to touch. He plugged away in nea

anonymity outside of the courtroom until 1997, when he defended Charles Price in federal court. Price had been convicted of violating the civil rights of a Hasidic man in Crown Heights in 1991 when he incited an attack on Yankel Rosenbaum by shouting, "Let's get a Jew." He was also found guilty of inflicting at least two of the four fatal stab wounds delivered to Rosenbaum. Now he faced charges that he'd violated Rosenbaum's civil rights.

It was in 1998, though, that he really drew the attention and firepower of the media. He defended Corey Arthur against charges that he shot and killed his high school teacher. Ricco was attacked in the press for his vicious cross-examinations and his vilification of the victim.

Later that year, he defended Mohamed Sadeek Odeh, a co-conspirator in the August 1998 bombing of American embassies in Kenya and Tanzania. He represented Sammy "The Bull" Gravano when, based on allegations made by Richard "Iceman" Kuklinski, the district attorney brought charges against Gravano for killing a police officer. In 2005, Ricco had to step back from that case because of a conflict of interest; those charges are still pending.

Ricco continued to rack up clients the rest of the country despised. He took up the cause of a Pakastani, Uzair Paracha, whose father was a detainee at Guantanamo Bay. He represented Mohammed Azmath, who was seized on an Amtrak train in Texas on September 12, 2001.

Ricco defended Tarik Shah, Bronx jazz musician, whom prosecutors charged provided material support to terrorists and "committed himself to the path of holy war, to the oath of secrecy, and to abide by the directives of Al Qaeda." Throughout these cases, Ricco often told the press that the charges were made because of the anti-Muslim bias that possessed prosecutors and justice officials in this country since 9-11.

Ricco also represented Andre Cooper in the first death

penalty case presented in a Pennsylvania court since the reinstatement of capital punishment in 1988.

Ricco's defense spared Cooper from execution. He was sentenced to life in prison.

Though people might disagree with his tactics in the courtroom, no one could deny his captivating presence or his singular style. David Klinghoffer described him as a natty retro dresser in the *National Review*: "the immaculately pressed tan suit and bow tie combination, accessorized by matching Homburg and black half-frame Malcolm X glasses . . . made the attorney look like he escaped from a 1940s hard-boiled detective novel." He went on to add, "if I can track down a suit like Anthony Ricco's, I'll be in Heaven."

Now, Anthony Ricco, in all of his sartorial splendor, stood at the side of Dean Faiello—a phony doctor, a drug abuser, a fugitive from justice and an accused murderer. What tricks would pop out of Ricco's bag this time?

CHAPTER THIRTY-NINE

THE MEDIA RAISED QUESTIONS ABOUT THE FORENSIC EVIdence discovered in Dean's Jeep Grand Cherokee. Police spokesman Michael Coan said, "We were aware of the car and determined that it was of no investigative value." Jeane MacIntosh and Brad Hamilton consulted with forensics experts. Lawrence Koblinsky, at John Jay College and a consultant for NYPD, said, "In my opinion, they screwed up. If he transported her, the car is considered one of the crime scenes. A good defense attorney could argue that the police were sloppy."

Another expert agreed, saying that it still wasn't a waste of time at this late date to search the vehicle— evidence could still be found. "Maybe a hair, a fiber, traces of a drug, who knows?"

DR. LAURIE POLIS AT LAST RECEIVED A CALL FROM THE district attorney's office. *About time*, she thought. Polis cooperated fully, providing them with all the information she had on Dean Faiello. Still, she avoided interviews with the media. She did not want to be a part of any article or story in connection with him.

Both of Dean's June court dates were postponed. Ronda Lustman of the Criminal Prosecution Bureau of the attorney general's office represented the state in the

case against Dean for unauthorized practice of medicine
She had hoped Dean would be sentenced for that crime
and that she could put away her Faiello file. Now, i
looked as if it would hang in limbo for a while.

It didn't appear as though Dean would be sentenced or
that charge until the murder trial. His time spent in custody awaiting trial would count as time served for any
sentence issued for the un-licensed practice of medicine
charge. At Dean's homicide trial, Lustman expected, the
judge would order what remained of those four years to
be served concurrently with the sentence he received on
the murder count, when and if Dean was convicted of
killing Maria Cruz.

DEAN NOW RESIDED ON RIKERS ISLAND IN THE EAST RIVER
New York City purchased the 90-acre hunk of land in
1884. Used as a sanitary landfill, the island grew to 400
acres with the addition of discarded remnants from the
large, growing metropolis. The city erected the first jail
on Rikers in the 1930s. In 2006, its ten major jails housed
more than 16,000 inmates. Dean's unit, the George R.
Vierno Center, named after the retired chief of the corrections department, opened in 1991 as an 850-bed facility.
In 1993, an addition to the center added room for another
500 prisoners.

"I try to keep busy reading one book in English and
one book in Spanish at all times, but it's not easy." Dean
said. "Rikers Island has no library, no book cart and
frowns upon prisoners reading books."

From the tiny window of his cell in the maximum security unit, Dean had a view of chain-link fence topped with
razor wire and the back side of a gray housing unit. "There
are no trees visible, no plants, no grass, no people and
nothing living," he wrote. "There are no colors except

gray." Almost the entire day, he listened to the annoying thrum of a large pump ten feet from his cell.

For 90 minutes each day, however, he got to leave his housing unit to go the law library. He had one hour of recreation time in a concrete courtyard without trees or grass. There was nothing to do out there but run in circles on the hard slab—no exercise equipment, no recreation or sports supplies for games of any sort and no radios or books were allowed.

Inside, the entertainment options available were not aligned with Dean's tastes at all. The TV showed an endless stream of gangster rap movies starring people like 50 Cent, martial arts films with Jet Li and mass annihilation flicks like *The Hills Have Eyes*—not one Oscar contender in the bunch. In between movies, the TV displayed concerts with Ja Rule and Ludacris. "I can see why he calls himself Ludacris," Dean wrote. "It describes his performance art perfectly."

While movies were on, he worked on crossword puzzles from newspapers—"The *New York Times'* are my favorites," he wrote.

The food, at least, was a dramatic improvement over Costa Rican jail fare. He gained back the weight he lost there and an additional twenty pounds besides. Health care was better, too. He started a regimen of antiretroviral treatment and lost his chronic cough and wheezing.

He wrote a stack of letters to the warden, deputies, commissioners, priests and even Attorney General Eliot Spitzer to decry the discrimination against Catholics and all Christians on Rikers Island. "The preferred religion here is Islam and those who are not Islamic are ignored." Dean wanted to participate in weekly mass and in Catholic Bible study classes, but was denied attendance. No one responded to his letters. "Pleas from non-Muslims in the correction system fall on deaf ears," he wrote.

Once a week, Dean, like the other prisoners in his unit, stood outside his cell in his underwear clutching his plastic mattress to his chest as corrections officers in riot gear conducted a search. They "invade every cell and tear apart everything that isn't bolted to the floor. They examine minutely every book, sheet of paper, magazines, sneakers, shirts, socks, underwear, linens, correspondence, medications, toilet paper and plastic cups and forks." Returning to his cell, Dean's belongings were scattered willy-nilly on top of his denuded metal cot. "And this goes on every week, month after month, until the process becomes dehumanizing and desensitizing."

After years of living well beyond his means, Dean Faiello claimed that the only money he now had was the $10 he received each week in prison salary.

ON JULY 25, 2005, DEAN LEFT HIS DREARY CELL ON RIKERS Island to appear in Manhattan Criminal Court. He carried a paperback copy of *Harry Potter and the Chamber of Secrets* in his manacled hands.

Ann Prunty announced that the grand jury handed down the official indictment, charging Dean with the crime of murder in the second degree. The document she filed read:

> The defendant, in the County of New York, on or about April 13, 2002, under circumstances evincing a depraved indifference to human life, recklessly engaged in conduct which created a grave risk of death to another person, and thereby caused the death of Maria Cruz.

Dean faced a sentence of 25 years to life on this charge.

On hearing the news, Rudolfo Cruz, from his home in Paranaque City, told the *Filipino Reporter*: "Thank God! The wheel of justice is grinding. We've been waiting for this moment." He added that he and his wife planned to fly to New York for the trial in October.

Dean returned to court on August 4 to enter his plea of not guilty. He was due in court again on October 19. When that day arrived, the court proceedings were moved forward to April 2006 because of conflicts in Ricco's court calendar.

That April, Rudolfo and Irenea flew to New York with their daughter, Dr. Tes Lara, and her husband, Tadeo, and two grandchildren, Isabel and Anton. They planned to attend Faiello's pre-trial hearing, staying at the Jersey City home of Maria's aunt, Rebecca de los Angeles.

Ricco, however, was not available in April either. Two death penalty cases created conflicts in his schedule. One was the trial in Pennsylvania. The other was the New York defense of Rudy Fleming, accused of murdering actress Nicole duFresne.

Although disappointed at the rescheduling of Dean's court date, the Cruz family accepted the reality with stoicism. Rudolfo told the *Filipino Reporter* that the family would fly back to New York for legal proceedings as many times as needed. "It could be costly, I know, but we'll do anything for Pipay," he said. "I will keep coming back until I am assured that Faiello will never see the light of day. I leave it up to the U.S. justice system and God. Ultimately, God, the one who knows everything, will be Faiello's final judge."

"My only worry," his wife Irenea added, "is that I may not be able to stand seeing Faiello face-to-face."

While in New York, the family met with Ann Prunty and other officials with the Manhattan district attorney's office. They also spent time with Leopoldo Abad, whose firm was handling Maria's estate, including her stocks and her savings accounts.

WHILE DEAN'S SELF-CENTERED FOCUS LED HIM DOWN A PATH of destruction, his former lover Jason Opsahl's giving nature built a legacy that helped others, even after his death. *Broadway Bares*—the charitable fundraiser inspired by Jason—hit the stage for the sixteenth time on Father's Day, 2006. What started as a grassroots effort by a handful of committed men now involved the volunteer services of hundreds of people each year. The show raised $650,950 for BC/EFA that night, bringing the total amount of funds donated since the show's inception to more than three-and-a-half million dollars.

BY THE SUMMER OF 2006, DEAN HAD BEEN IN THE CUSTODY OF the corrections system in New York for more than a year. The season arrived in full force in New York City. Muggy air wrapped warm, wet tendrils around its occupants. Many found relief in their air-conditioned homes. For those on Rikers Island, however, there was no relief—no air conditioning, no fans, very little ventilation at all.

The small windows in Dean's cell opened just a crack, providing a barely perceptible movement of air. Dean stopped going outside to run on the hot concrete. When his recreation hour arrived, he remained in his small hole, where the air was hot, humid and still. "All I do all day is sweat, work on crossword puzzles and read," he wrote. "I have fallen into a slump both physically and mentally."

Dean's trial date was set for September 7, 2006. Greg Bach, although on the official list of witnesses for the state, did not expect to be called to testify. The bridges between himself and the prosecution were burned beyond repair. He did not trust them and suspected that they shared the feeling.

Greg wanted to move on with his life—and he tried. But the shadow of his past with Dean darkened every day. He hoped to return to the creative expression of sand sculpting in the summer of 2006. Life had been on hold for far too long.

He tried to get past his feelings of anger about the whole situation. "After all," he said, "my losses pale when compared to the anguish of the Cruz family. It's so sad, though, for everyone. I have an overall feeling of heartbreak for so many people." Greg felt wounded by the way he was treated by Dean and his family. He still felt the pain of the attacks by Detective Della Rocca and Assistant District Attorney Ann Prunty. He also felt his own family's distress, and their growing concern for him.

He insisted he had no knowledge of Maria Cruz's death at the time it occurred. He knew he played no role in the cover-up. Someone must have known, though, he thought. It seemed unlikely that Dean would not feel compelled to confide in at least one person. Greg surely hadn't been Dean's confidant. If Dean had told him, Greg would have given him an ultimatum: "Either you turn yourself in or I'll do it for you." Dean must have known he would react that way.

There were rumors that Mark Ritchey knew—that he was complicit in the hiding of Maria's body. Greg dismissed that speculation. He didn't believe Mark was capable of being that callous.

Then there was Patty Rosado. Did Dean tell her in the spring or summer of 2003? Did she figure it out on her own long before Maria's body was found? Patty hacked into Dean's computer. She reviewed all of Dean's files. She was the first person Dean called on the night of April 13, 2003. She was the last person to shelter him before he fled to Costa Rica. Did Patty use her knowledge to leverage Dean into a sexual relationship? Had she believed that keeping his secret would bind him to her forever?

Many hoped that during the trial all secrets and machinations would be revealed. They awaited Dean's appearance in court on October 16, 2006.

Ireana and Rodolfo Cruz flew into New York from the Philippines on October 15. They watched as Dean entered New York County Supreme Court wearing jeans, a short-sleeved shirt and a few more pounds on his once-thin frame. Dean stood by his attorney, Anthony Ricco, and faced Judge Gregory Carro.

Carro asked if he wanted to plead guilty to assault in the first degree "under conditions evincing depraved indifference to human life."

"Yes, Your Honor," Dean said.

"Is it true that at that time you were addicted to cocaine and were a heavy user?"

"That's correct," Dean answered, adding that he was under the influence of cocaine when Maria arrived at his illegal clinic for laser surgery on her tongue.

"You gave her an injection?" the judge asked.

Ireana sobbed gently in the background of Dean's admission. "Yes, sir," he said. Then he admitted that when Maria's seizures began, he called his former neighbor and emergency room doctor David Goldschmitt for advice. The doctor urged him to take Maria to a hospital immediately.

"You ignored that advice?" Carro asked.

"Yes," Dean said, explaining that he was too frightened to face the consequences of continuing to practice medicine without a license.

Anthony Ricco and Manhattan Assistant District Attorney Ann Prunty negotiated a deal for Dean Faiello. In exchange for his guilty plea to first-degree assault, the state dropped the second-degree murder charge. Instead of facing 25 years to life in prison, Dean agreed to 20 years of jail time.

There would be no trial—no revelations—no answers to many of the remaining questions.

One irrefutable truth remained: Maria Cruz is dead—her young life snuffed out before its time in a needless, heedless moment. Tes Cruz Lara laid Maria's death at the doorstep of the United States: "I had no idea this could happen in America. I wanted to come here myself. After this, I cannot come here. I cannot live here and always remember my sister."

In her diary, Tes wrote to Maria:

"Someday I will see you once more. Until then I rest in your memories to keep you alive in my heart."

AFTERWORD

WITH THE DEATH OF MARIA CRUZ, WE AGAIN WITNESS THE lingering devastation of one person's murder. The tendrils of pain stretch beyond immediate family and friends to encompass and damage the lives of a long list of people whose paths directly or indirectly intersect with the crime.

It affects all of us. Each of us loses a little bit of our humanity with the unwarranted death of an individual. From Maria's loss, there are lessons to be learned—wisdom to be gained—a knowledge with the potential to protect our own lives and the lives of those we hold dear.

The most obvious is that substance abuse, whether through prescription drugs, illegal drugs or alcohol, is a road to destruction. Had Dean Faiello lived a life of relative sobriety, odds are he would have never made the bad choices that destroyed relationships, smashed his future and ultimately led to the death of another human being.

A bigger life lesson, though, is the danger we all face when we place the pursuit of exterior beauty over the maintenance of our own health. In 2004, phony doctor Luis Sanchez was sentenced to 5 years in prison for injecting hundreds of patients with industrial strength silicone. Two years after his conviction, many are still being treated for pain, scarring and disfigurement. When we value the least expensive option like Botox, silicon or collagen injections at a friend's house or services at a cut-rate makeshift office by someone with dubious credentials over the more expensive services of a trained professional, we put ourselves at serious risk.

The aging of the baby boomer generation has ushered in a greater acceptance of beauty procedures and cosmetic surgery. Laser machines popped up everywhere in response to consumer demand. Most operators are conscientious and trained. A minority—including licensed physicians who grabbed a laser and a weekend course— forge forward providing treatment with only money on their minds.

"Entrepreneurial types feel these procedures can be done by anyone," Dr. Roy Geronemus said. "But you need training in the problem as well as the device. You have to exercise clinical judgment, because lasers interact with the skin in different ways depending on the individual's age, skin type and color. It is not like a point-and-shoot camera."

For most boomers, removal of unwanted hair by laser or electrolysis is the only treatment they seek. For others, elective cosmetic surgery is a rare indulgence to satisfy a plummeting ego, enhance employment prospects or revitalize a relationship. There are those, however, who get as hooked on it as Dean got hooked on drugs. Obsessive reliance on these artificial body enhancements produces people like Michael Jackson, whose sculpted faces look more alien than human. The lesser known American socialite Joycelyn Wildenstein may be an even starker example of plastic surgery abuse than Jackson. After finding her husband in bed with a 21-year-old, Wildenstein reportedly spent more than three million dollars on cosmetic procedures. She has silicone injections in her lips, cheeks and chin, implants in her chin and lips, at least one face lift and eye reconstruction to make her resemble the large, wild cats her husband loved. Recently, a plastic surgery website dubbed her "the world's scariest celebrity."

For younger generations, facial surgery is seen as a preventative measure to slow the onset of wrinkles and sagging skin. The demand for breast augmentation is at an all-time high. Many younger women think only of improving their image and never stop to consider the long-term consequences of breast implants. Breast-feeding of a baby is eliminated as an option, a naturally erogenous zone is often numbed to sensation and, in all likelihood, the surgery will need to be repeated every ten years.

Maria Cruz had successful breast augmentation and facial surgery before she ever visited Dean Faiello. She apparently researched the physicians for those procedures very thoroughly. So why didn't she take the same care with Dean? When she didn't, she made herself vulnerable, as cosmetic surgery is the only field of medicine where invasive procedures are often pursued based on a self-diagnosis of need instead of on an objective medical assessment.

Even cosmetic surgery performed by a degreed medical professional comes with risks that we ignore at our own peril. Although the vast majority of doctors do not recklessly perform procedures without a thorough understanding of all the possible ramifications, there are twisted practitioners who have forsaken their oaths in the pursuit of a dollar—physicians who take short cuts instead of obtaining in-depth training, some of whom are not even competent to practice. It is vital to check the professional standing of any new doctor before undergoing any procedure at his hand.

Kay Kelly Cregan of County Cork, Ireland, came to

Manhattan for an ordinary face lift. After reading a positive article in her local newspaper about the celebrity clients of Dr. Michael Sachs, she entrusted her life to his care and looked no further.

She most likely would have selected another physician if she had better researched his record. In less than ten years, Sachs had settled thirty lawsuits for botched operations—more than any other doctor in the state of New York. Hours after her procedure, Cregan went into cardiac arrest. She died two days later on St. Patrick's Day, 2004.

That same year, Olivia Goldsmith, author of *The First Wives Club*, visited the Manhattan Eye, Ear and Throat Hospital for a chin tuck. She, too, experienced cardiac arrest, slipped into a coma and died. The state health department fined the hospital $20,000 for a serious breakdown in patient care.

The year these two women died, there were more than 1.9 million cosmetic surgical procedures performed in the United States. Most of them were done to the patients' satisfaction and without serious detrimental effects to their health. To the families of Kay and Olivia, however, the success stories of others pale in comparison to the loss that darkens every day of their lives.

The most important thing to remember when seeking one of these treatments is that elective surgery is never an emergency. Take the time to research your physician. Finding the right doctor can be a byzantine effort and accessing a doctor's record is often a convoluted process.

In some states, a system has evolved to provide easy access to needed information on line. In others, it is necessary to grapple with a bureaucracy that obstructs or delays full public disclosure. No matter how complex the task, don't proceed with any elective surgery without knowing your doctor's record.

You also need to be certain your doctor really has the credentials he claims. Watch for red flags—anything that indicates an abnormal medical process. If you visit a person claiming to be a dermatologist or plastic surgeon and you are whisked through with minimal paperwork, be concerned. An ethical physician will be certain to obtain extensive medical history, provide you with information on exactly what will be done, let you know what to expect afterwards and give you a clear understanding of any risks you may face. When asked to sign an informed consent document, don't do so until you have a genuine awareness of what lies ahead. Every invasive procedure—every anesthetic—carries a risk. If your questions are not receiving thorough and satisfactory answers, head for the door.

The practitioners who claim to be licensed physicians and are not create yet another trap for the unwary. Dean Faiello did so verbally, but others take it even further. They plaster "M.D." after their names, steal school records and medical credentials from real doctors and advertise board certifications they do not possess.

The most notorious fake, Gerald Barnes, pretended to be a doctor for more than twenty years after attaining the documentation of a real doctor with the same name. His ruse was so perfectly executed, he contracted with the federal government to provide physicals for FBI agents in Los Angeles without being caught in his scam. Barnes was arrested and served sentences in jail more than once. After every release from prison, he resumed his medical practice. Now, at the age of 73, he is serving time for his fifth conviction for practicing medicine without a license.

He is only one of many people impersonating doctors in hospitals, clinics and private practice. David Tremoglie saw more than 500 patients and wrote thousands of prescriptions as a psychiatrist at a mental health clinic in Pennsylvania. He served 3 years in jail. In the same state, Douglas Lenhart went to prison in 2004 for attempting the castration of a transgendered woman in her dining room. Dennis Roark treated more than a thousand patients in Michigan and assisted in hundreds of surgeries—including heart bypass operations—before he was caught and sentenced to 6 to 14 years behind bars.

According to Ronda Lustman of the attorney general's office in New York, "There is a lot of illegal practice in New York with the highest concentration in Chinatown. Much of what we see involves fraudulent diplomas from the Dominican Republic and forged credentials from medical school." In fact, investigators in New York found 580 cases of phony doctors practicing medicine in a four-year period. In Florida, the Department of Health created an unlicensed activity office in 1998. In fiscal year 2003, they investigated 765 complaints and scored 101 convictions for the unlicensed practice of medicine.

Contact state officials to confirm that your doctor is licensed to practice medicine. Do it every time you need the services of a new physician. Just because they are in business doesn't mean they have a right to be.

Many of the perpetrators are caught not by something they've done in their practice, but by how they reacted in a situation where the unexpected occurred and a crisis developed. Dean Faiello panicked instead of getting the appropriate treatment for Maria. He then took the situation to an extreme, burying her body and concealing her death.

In the cosmetics industry, the problem goes beyond practitioners falsely representing themselves as doctors. There's also an issue with technicians who, without claiming any false credentials, perform procedures for which they are not qualified. The problem often lies in the way legal definitions are written.

"Technology," Lustman said, "has outstripped the law." In most states, the statutes governing the use of lasers are vague and confusing—to physicians, technicians and the public alike. In New York, laser hair removal clearly does not require a medical license and oblative—or invasive—laser procedures demand it. In between, there is a gray area of undefined services. Also open to interpretation is the meaning of a doctor's supervision when mandated by law. New York is not the only state where no black-and-white standards are spelled out in existing regulations.

Many licensed dermatologists and plastic surgeons in New York want the use of lasers in treatment to be the sole prerogative of licensed physicians, as it is in some states. They claim that laser technology has become increasingly complex and advanced. These strides in technology make a laser in the hands of a non–medical operator a danger to the public. Roy Geronemus said that mishaps at dozens of spas in Manhattan have sent a steady stream of patients to his office. He's treated models whose careers have been destroyed by burns from laser hair removal. One of his patients went to a spa for the removal of a mole. "She came into my office with a large scar on her lip. In addition to the scarring, there were serious medical concerns. No biopsy was performed, so there was no way to know whether cancer was present or not."

Unfortunately, it is difficult from anecdotal evidence to assess how much real danger exists and how much is due to the conflict of interest physicians face. There are those who are motivated solely by concerns for the public welfare. Others, however, are more focused on financial interest when they express a desire to make the use of laser as restrictive as possible. "Doctors want to own the beauty industry," cosmetic technician Muriel Farina said.

"They want you to come to them for laser hair removal, and facials so that they can upgrade you to something even costlier like Botox injections and surgery. It's all about money."

Technicians like Muriel point out that electrolysis is a far more invasive procedure than laser hair removal, and a medical degree has never been required for the practice of electrology. In fact, many states do not have proficiency testing or licensure of electrologists. Technicians insist that although a doctor is only necessary for oblative laser treatments when infection is a possibility—for example, the removal of spider angiomas, commonly known as spider veins—doctors are attempting to reserve the use of lasers exclusively for themselves with other less risky procedures. Procedures like facials, pimple punctures with sterile lances, microdermabrasion and electrology, they say, require training but not a medical education.

Where does the spin end and the truth begin? These technicians—like the doctors—are biased by their personal financial interests.

It is an issue that needs to be considered by an informed, disinterested third party. Only if legislators educate themselves on the technology, weigh the claims on both sides and ignore lobbyists can they draft laws that protect the public. With increasing numbers of Americans seeking these cosmetic services, the time for a thorough examination and clear, concise legislation is long past due.

Practitioners often skate the edges of legality because they do not understand existing laws. Then there are those who extend their services beyond what they know is legal—people like Dean Faiello, who look a prospective client in the eye and assure him of their medical qualifications; people who manage to pull it off because unethical physicians—like Andrew Reyner and Michael

Jackowitz—aid them in their deception by providing prescription drugs and protective cover.

How, though, could a woman like Maria Cruz be deceived? Highly educated and incredibly smart and knowledgeable about Internet research techniques, she seemed an unlikely client for a man like Dean Faiello.

Why didn't she check to see if he had a medical license? Why didn't she ferret out his arrest in October 2002? And if she did, why did she ignore the warning signs? Why didn't she run from him the moment he asked her to bring cash? If Maria knew the answers to these questions, she took them with her to her resting place.

And what motivated Dean Faiello? Greg Bach pointed to Dean's insatiable hunger for drugs, but also said, "There is a part of him that really thinks he is Dr. Faiello. I think he can disassociate from himself and believe his own lies because it is too painful to be him."

Criminal profiler Pat Brown has a harsher assessment. She said Dean Faiello was "a guy who always wants power and control—the usual hallmarks of psychopathy. He simply won't take himself out of the driver's seat. He practiced medicine illegally because he liked the powerful feeling he got from it. He got busted and continued to practice medicine because he liked the power.

"Everybody follows patterns. This guy has a history of not giving a damn what is right and wrong—both legally and ethically. He demonstrated little concern for anyone but himself in his past and in this crime." Because of his psychopathology, she surmised, when Maria Cruz became dangerously ill, he still placed his needs over those of his patient, and acted in his self-interest without a thought for hers.

Wherever Dean fits in this continuum—from an emotionally damaged man seeking admiration and respect, to a narcissist or psychopath who has no real regard for other individuals—he deliberately created an image for himself that took advantage of others' gullibility. He was part caring practitioner, part con artist. He is one of the handful of people in every profession whose corruption taints the whole system.

Barbara Nevins Taylor began an on-line essay about the nature of evil with these remarks:

> Until a few years ago, I believed that we were all basically good. It seemed to me that most of us, given a little time to think about things, would make the right decisions and behave ethically. Foolish me.
>
> Every day as I investigate one scheme or another, I meet people who are bad, maybe even evil. They are schemers who recognize that people with dreams will believe the most implausible stories simply because they hope that their dreams will come true.

She wrapped up the piece with a warning:

> We've found that people who get ripped off in any scheme often step into the traps that are set for them with their eyes half closed. They don't do research about a company, or a contractor, and they are often eager to do things quickly, cheaply and easily.
>
> Unfortunately, they end up learning the hard way and costly way that the bad guys have no conscience when it comes to taking advantage of their vulnerability, making promises for things they will not deliver and taking their money.

From doctors to roofers, be sure you know in whom you're entrusting your life, your health, your cash. Protect yourself from victimization by doing your homework and questioning everything.

In the oft-repeated words of *Hill Street Blues*' Sergeant Phil Esterhaus at the end of every roll call: "And hey, let's be careful out there."

You can do it—for yourself, your loved ones, your friends. I know you can.